# PAUL

PAUL
Narrative or Apocalyptic

Cover image: Savanah N. Landerholm
Cover design: Photo by Souradeep Biswas on Unsplash

Print ISBN: 978-1-5064-8808-0
eBook ISBN: 978-1-5064-8809-7

# CONTENTS

Paul's Apocalyptic Theology    1
*J. Christiaan Beker*

Paul's Narrative Hope    71
*N. T. Wright*

# PAUL'S APOCALYPTIC THEOLOGY

*Apocalyptic and the Resurrection of Christ*

## J. Christiaan Beker

THIS ESSAY WILL discuss the basic framework of Paul's thought and determine its coherent center. It argues that Paul's thought is anchored in the apocalyptic world view and that the resurrection of Christ can only be understood in that setting. The interpretation of 1 Corinthians 15 will back that claim. The argument rejects those construals of Paul's thought that suppress, delimit, or compromise its apocalyptic texture. In that context the interpretative bias against apocalyptic in the history of doctrine will be criticized, a bias that until recently has dominated the treatment of apocalyptic.

The coherent center of Paul's gospel is constituted by the apocalyptic interpretation of the Christ-event. "Paul's outlook is at bottom that of Jewish apocalyptic. While conceptions from other sources . . . have to be taken into account, they are superimposed on an apocalyptic groundwork."[1]

First I will discuss what apocalyptic is and how Paul is related to that movement.

## The Apocalyptic World View

Philipp Vielhauer[2] and Klaus Koch[3] have outlined the basic components of apocalyptic as a movement of thought. For Vielhauer this includes:

1. The doctrine of the two ages with its radical dualism.
2. Pessimism and otherworldly hope, which expresses the fundamental thought of apocalyptic dualism, that is, the radical discontinuity between this age and the coming age.

3. Universalism and individualism, that is, the cosmic, universal scope of apocalyptic and its view of the person as no longer a member of a collective entity.
4. Determinism and imminent expectation of the kingdom of God, which involves God's prefixed plan of history, calculations about the end of history, and its periodization (four, seven, or twelve periods).[4]

Koch gives a more comprehensive picture which differs in many ways from Vielhauer's:

1. An urgent expectation of the impending overthrow of all earthly conditions in the immediate future.
2. The end appears as a vast cosmic catastrophe.
3. The time of this world is divided into segments.
4. The introduction of an army of angels and demons to explain the course of historical events and the happenings of the end time.
5. Beyond the catastrophe a new salvation arises, paradisal in character and destined for the faithful remnant.
6. The transition from disaster to final redemption takes place by means of an act issuing from the throne of God, which means the visibility on earth of the kingdom of God.
7. The frequent introduction of a mediator with royal functions.
8. "The catchword *glory* is used wherever the final state of affairs is set apart from the present and whenever a final amalgamation of the earthly and heavenly spheres is prophesied."[5]

Koch's interpretation is preferable to Vielhauer's because it is more precise and more critical. He deplores the usual ascription to apocalyptic of radical dualism, otherworldly utopianism, remote transcendence of God, and utter determinism and suggests instead the components of continuity, of the hidden presence of the kingdom, and of history as a meaningful process.

From these descriptions one can deduce that apocalyptic revolves around three basic ideas: (1) historical dualism; (2) universal cosmic expectation; and (3) the imminent end of the world. However, a systematic description of apocalyptic should not deceive us into viewing it as a purely speculative and abstract phenomenon. To the contrary, apocalyptic is born out of a deep existential concern and is in many respects a theology of martyrdom. The apocalyptist has a profound awareness of the discrepancy between what is and what should be, and of the tragic tension between faithfulness to the Torah and its apparent futility. Therefore, he lives a hope that seems contradicted by the realities of his world but that is fed by his faith in the faithfulness of the God of Israel and his ultimate self-vindication. Will God keep his promises to his people and reward their faithfulness to the covenant? Will he, notwithstanding present persecution, establish his people in victory over their enemies and thus vindicate his glory in the glorious destiny of his people? Contrary to a long trend in scholarship that since Julius Wellhausen[6] has viewed apocalyptic as speculative armchair academics and as a degeneration of Israel's prophetic religion, apocalyptic is not to be understood without the existential realities of martyrdom, persecution, moral fiber, and encouragement and the longing for a final theodicy. The discontinuity between this age and the age to come points to a radical transformation of the present world order, because the world is presently ruled by Satan, death, and the forces of evil. This dialectic of negation and affirmation is accompanied by a sense of imminent expectation of God's universal reign. The cry of imminent expectation: "O Sovereign Lord, holy and true, how long before thou wilt judge and avenge our blood on those who dwell upon the earth?" (Rev. 6:10) is conjoined to the universal-cosmic hope of "a new heaven and a new earth" (Rev. 21:1).

In this context we must correct some basic misconceptions about apocalyptic. It is erroneous to play off "Pharisaic" Judaism against

4 J. Christiaan Beker

"apocalyptic" Judaism, as if both constituted distinct "parties" in Palestinian Judaism with quite different conceptions of the law.[7] This distinction has become popular since the classic works of George Foot Moore[8] and Wilhelm Bousset.[9] Moore depicted first-century Judaism along the lines of "normative" Judaism (i.e., the Tannaite tradition after Jamnia [A.D. 90], when Pharisaism became the norm for Jewish religion). Bousset, to the contrary, stressed the "popular" religion of the times as opposed to "legalistic" Pharisaism and assigned a predominant role to apocalyptic conventicles. This division in scholarship is still operative in the work of Dietrich Rössler,[10] who opposes a rabbinic casuistic observance of the Torah to its apocalyptic salvation-historical conception. He views the Torah in an apocalyptic context as the domain of God's faithful covenantal pledge to Israel. Especially since the discovery of Qumran, the pervasive apocalyptic character of pre-Jamnia Judaism has been increasingly recognized. Apocalyptic fervor no doubt inspired the movement behind the Jewish war of A.D. 66–70, which was supported by the Pharisees. Josephus tells us of a series of messianic movements that attempted to overthrow the Roman occupation[11] (cf. also Theudas and Judas the Galilean in Acts 5:36–37). The Zealots, the Sicarii, and the Qumran community are inexplicable without this apocalyptic fervor, and The War Scroll testifies to the (Essene) preparedness for the final eschatological battle against "the children of darkness." Because it was this apocalyptic stimulant that according to the fathers of Jamnia had been responsible for the war and the destruction of Jerusalem, they purged and/or softened the apocalyptic element from the Mishna (A.D. 180) and became exceedingly cautious about apocalyptic speculation. Louis Ginsburg gives a good example of the new sobriety of the rabbis after the war: "If thou hast a sapling in thy hands and thou art told: Behold, the Messiah has come, plant thy sapling and then go to meet him" (R. Johanan ben Zakkai).[12] In this early article (1922) Ginsburg cautions against a split between "Pharisaic" and "apocalyptic" Judaism: "It would be very difficult to prove the contention that the attitude of the apocalyptic authors toward the Torah was different from that taken by the Rabbis."[13] It is only after the wars of A.D. 70 and A.D. 132 that "normative" Judaism excises its apocalyptic components. However, as I have shown (see Chapter 9 in my *Paul the Apostle*), the relative weight of "apocalyptic" as compared to "rabbinic" must be acknowledged in the period before Jamnia, for the multiformity of the Judaism of the Second Commonwealth is obvious and does not allow us simply to fuse rabbinic and apocalyptic traditions and groups[14] or to make Second Commonwealth rabbinic Judaism the norm of pre-Jamnia Judaism.[15]

It is also an error to make a hard-and-fast division between so-called messianism and apocalypticism, as if the former is nationalistic and confined to Israel with a Davidic messiah as warlord and conqueror who will subject the enemies of Israel to his throne in Jerusalem, and the latter is transcendental and universalistic. To be sure, apocalypticism often comprises a universal history that concerns the rise and fall of world empires and expects a cosmic redemption that will be inaugurated by a preexistent redeemer figure.[16] Although there are remarkable differences between, for instance, the eschatological picture of the Psalms of Solomon and 4 Ezra or the Apocalypse of Baruch, the nature of apocalyptic does not allow its stock of images to be classified along nationalistic or cosmic-universal lines. In the vision of Judaism, the eschatological hope is intertwined with miraculous, cosmic happenings, and universal cosmic expectations of God's intervention regularly blend with "national" messianic figures. This has been characteristic of apocalyptic thinking from its early appearance in Isaiah 24–27, Zechariah, and Daniel, and it is apparent in Qumran with its twin messianic figures.

Dualism, the cosmic rule of God, and the hope of its imminent coming form the crux of apocalyptic thought. It is, however, erroneous to press dualism into a blatant unconcern for this world or to interpret the hope in God's imminent rule as an escape from ethical responsibility. Although there is disagreement about these issues in scholarship, we will see that Paul's apocalyptic cannot be thus interpreted.

## The Interpretation of Apocalyptic Eschatology

It must be pointed out that the interpretation of the future eschatological dimension of the hope has been largely a stream of misinterpretation in the history of the church. To be sure, both Albert Schweitzer and Martin Werner have drawn attention to the de-eschatologizing of the early Christian message in the history of the church.[17] However, their basic insights have until recently been neglected by systematic theology and biblical scholarship alike. The history of futurist eschatology in the church has been one long process of spiritualization and/or ecclesiologizing or institutionalizing, especially under the influence of Origen and Augustine. From the condemnation of Montanism in the second century and the exclusion of chiliastic apocalypticism at the Council of Ephesus (A.D. 431) through its condemnation by the reformers (in the Augsburg Confession) and until today, future eschatology was pushed out of the mainstream of church life and thus pushed into heretical aberrations. The impact of this spiritualizing process and the distaste for apocalyptic speculations made by sectarian groups have no doubt contributed to the overwhelmingly negative estimate of apocalyptic by biblical and theological scholarship since the Enlightenment.

It is necessary to gain a more adequate and historical view of apocalyptic in view of a long tradition of antiapocalyptic sentiment. From Julius Wellhausen and Bernhard Duhm[18] until recent times, apocalyptic has been vilified as armchair sophistry, degeneration of prophecy, utopian speculation, ethical passivity, and so on. In 1959, Rudolf Schnackenburg can still claim:

> *This dwelling on fantastic nightmares, this conscious excitement of anxiety and fear, this deliberate indulgence in an emotional expectation of the end of the world, coupled with the hammering on the theme of apocalyptic's secret knowledge . . . its concealment from the multitude and its delivery to the wise . . . the pride of the elect and the contempt for the* massa damnata—*indeed the positive thirst*

*for revenge and pleasure in the destruction of the wicked: all*
*these things are a heavy shadow on the picture, otherwise so*
*radiant, of universal perfection; and they are a blot on the*
*apocalyptic writers who created them.*[19]

Thus it comes as no surprise that Neoorthodoxy collapsed apocalyptic eschatology into Christology. "Eschatological" was no longer an ontic event expected in the future but a noetic-hermeneutical tool, that is, a linguistic concept, defining Christology as God's ultimate revelatory word. In the modern era the world view of the Enlightenment has shaped the hermeneutic of future eschatology in a threefold way: (1) the demything by historical-critical liberalism; (2) the demythologizing by the Bultmann school that has its roots in David Friedrich Strauss's conception of myth;[20] (3) the solution of realized eschatology, popularized by Charles Harold Dodd.[21] I mention this broad movement of the spiritualization and excision of apocalyptic eschatology because it has greatly influenced Pauline scholarship and has caused a misconstrual of the eschatological hope in Paul's thought. It has contributed to a wrong hermeneutic of Pauline thought, as if apocalyptic was a vestige on the periphery of Paul's theology. Liberal interpreters of the past considered the apocalyptic framework an ornamental husk that could be removed without affecting the core of Paul's thought. William Morgan speaks for many when he states:

*In expositions designed for edification it is inevitable that the*
*original framework, foreign as it has to a large extent become,*
*should be for the most part discounted and that the apostle's*
*central ideas should receive a more modern setting. With such*
*procedure no fault can be found; and that it is possible is a*
*proof that these ideas are at bottom of permanent validity.*

The dimension of the apocalyptic hope is here a framework that is in any event peripheral to Paul's timeless "central ideas."[22]

Rudolf Bultmann, to the contrary, deserves merit for recognizing the arbitrary method of liberalism in picking and choosing between husk and core. He posits that the whole of Paul's thought occurs within an apocalyptic-mythical world view and that therefore all Paul's thought must be reinterpreted or demythologized.[23] Bultmann subjects Paul to an existential interpretation, that is, an interpretation in terms of the anthropological self-understanding that myth contains. The cosmological-futurist elements of myth constitute obsolete and misleading language when interpreted literally, and they are to be read anthropologically. Thus, the apocalyptic myth intends to speak about the transcendence of God, "who is always the One, who comes to us from outside our known and manageable world."[24]

> *The understanding of Christian existence as a life in which God is always one who comes and as a life which is always a future possibility is—of course—not always fully explicit in the New Testament in all its ramifications. In fact, there was at the outset a serious obstacle to its full realization. The obstacle was the eschatology which the early church took over from Judaism, with its expectation of an imminent end of the world and the ushering in of ultimate salvation by a cosmic catastrophe. Only the author of the Fourth Gospel has emancipated himself from this eschatology. But when Paul says that faith, hope and love remain even when "that which is perfect" is come [1 Cor. 13:13], he is bringing an important truth to light. This is, that if real life means being open to the future, it can never be regarded as a definitive state of bliss. Faith and hope are the dispositions of those who are always looking for the grace of God as a future possibility.[25]*

Radical openness for the future means "that we are always in via, that we have never reached the end."

*We may—it is true—still find in the New Testament,*
*including the Pauline writings, the Jewish belief in the*
*transcendent glory as the compensation for suffering in this*
*world [e.g., Rom. 8:18–25; 2 Cor. 4:17–18], but for Paul*
*such a belief has lost its motive power.*[26]

Although Bultmann criticizes the liberal interpretation of apocalyptic myth, he likewise surrenders the integrity of Paul's thought, although in a more sophisticated way. Both Morgan and Bultmann adopt a stance toward myth that contrasts the scientific world view with the world of myth and seeks to rob apocalyptic myth of its cosmic-historical intent. The real stumbling blocks of Paul's apocalyptic world view for modern mentality are here conveniently removed, that is, the dimensions of imminence and cosmic-universal expectation. In fact, Bultmann can do justice only to the dualistic dimension of Paul's apocalyptic world view. This dimension is easily open to a spiritualism of "the finite over against the infinite" or to a scheme of spiritual transcendence. Thus, in Bultmann's *New Testament Theology* the "not yet" of eschatological hope is interpreted as the permanently valid dialectical opposite of the "already," that is, as man's utter dependence on the transcendent God[27] (see Chapter 12 in my *Paul the Apostle*). The chronological dimension between the present and the future is to be understood not in temporal but in existential terms, something the post-Pauline writings failed to do.[28] Bultmann's interpretation of Paul, however impressive, is essentially a Johannine interpretation, and it is no surprise that the only commentary Bultmann has written is on the Gospel of John. The demise of apocalyptic categories in John's spiritualistic interpretation of the Christ-event is, as it were, imported into Paul. Hermeneutically, Bultmann arranges apocalyptic under the general category of myth and opposes a literal understanding of myth to its anthropological intent. However, he ignores the historic-cosmic intent of the apocalyptic world view, and the antithesis between literal and figurative speech now becomes a denial of the realistic intent of the language.[29] The language of apocalyptic myth is more than an existentialist projection of man's plight because it concerns the reality of the cosmic victory of the creator over his created world.

John Goodrich Gager[30] detects a similar anthropological function in Paul's apocalyptic language about the end time. He points out that end-time language often functions either to exhort Christians to moral behavior or to console them in their present afflictions (cf., e.g., 1 Cor. 6:9, 10; Gal. 5:21; Rom. 8:18–25; and 2 Cor. 4:1—5:10). There is no question that these hortative conclusions do exist at the end of apocalyptic sections (cf. 1 Thess. 4:18; 5:11; 1 Cor. 15:58). However, there is a question as to whether these exhortations and consolations are the primary function of the apocalyptic sections or whether they must be seen as belonging to a wider cosmological context that is part of Paul's world view. Demything and demythologizing, then, seriously jeopardize the integrity of Paul's thought. Paul's language is here interpreted as in need of correction, and we must either disregard the language (Morgan) or reinterpret its "literal" character (Bultmann). To be sure, a "literal" reading of apocalyptic images (in Evangelical and Pentecostal circles) derives from a modernistic, denotative conception of language and thus signifies a distortion of apocalyptic in the scientific mood. However, the question remains whether the alternative to the "literal" is the "existential" (anthropological), because the category of the "literal" threatens to become a convenient instrument to amputate Paul's intent. The relation between the literal and the real in apocalyptic language is too easily solved in terms of a spiritualistic interpretation.

The solution of "realized eschatology" is subject to a similar verdict, for here a unilinear developmental scheme is introduced into the Pauline letters and is subsequently used to deapocalypticize Paul's thought. A primitive apocalyptic stage (1 Thessalonians) is opposed to the "divine commonwealth" stage of Paul's maturity (Ephesians), so that the apocalyptic-future hope is eliminated in favor of a realized eschatology in the later Paul. This scheme assumes the authenticity of

Colossians and Ephesians and neglects the fact that all the Pauline letters were composed in a very short period (A.D. 50–56), which makes any extensive revision of Pauline thought patterns unlikely. Furthermore, future apocalyptic references in late letters like Galatians (5:5), Romans (13:11), and Philippians (3:21) resist any such major revision (see Chapter 3 in my *Paul the Apostle*).

"Eschatology" in Neoorthodoxy becomes a term that no longer has any precise meaning; it is usually opposed to the "bad" term "apocalyptic" and signifies the transcendent, ultimate character of the Christ-event as God's new self-revelation. When Karl Barth writes that "if Christianity be not altogether thoroughgoing eschatology, there remains in it no relationship whatever with Christ,"[31] the term "thoroughgoing eschatology" refers not to future eschatology but to the Christ-event as God's transcendent revelation, which is and remains God's alone and touches history only tangentially. Resurrection is now defined as *Ewigkeit im Nu*. The early Barth is a Christomonist for whom Christology swallows up future eschatology. Paul Althaus's evaluation of apocalyptic is typical of that held by many theologians:

> *The world has in principle its end in the judgment and the kingdom in Christ. In this sense every time in history and likewise history as a whole, is an end-time, because both individually and as a whole it borders upon eternity and has an immediate relation to its judgment and its redemption.* To this extent all the hours of history are the self-same last hour.[32] *[Emphasis mine.]*

To be sure, the post-Bultmannian period has reversed in many ways this low estimate of apocalyptic in theology and biblical scholarship. Theologians like Jürgen Moltmann and Wolfhart Pannenberg,[33] biblical scholars like Ernst Käsemann, Peter Stuhlmacher,[34] and others express a new appreciation for apocalyptic and its positive contribution for understanding early Christianity and Paul in a new way (see

Chapter 2 in my *Paul the Apostle*). Käsemann's thesis—"apocalyptic was the mother of all Christian theology"[35]—opened up a new era of interpretation. As Klaus Koch says:

> *Up to then apocalyptic had been for biblical scholarship*
> *something on the periphery of the Old and New*
> *Testaments—something bordering on heresy. Käsemann had*
> *suddenly declared that a tributary was the main stream, from*
> *which everything else at the end of the Old Testament and the*
> *beginning of the New was allegedly fed.*[36]

It is my intent to press this new appreciation of apocalyptic for a fresh understanding of Paul, because only a consistent apocalyptic interpretation of Paul's thought is able to demonstrate its fundamental coherence.

## Paul and Apocalyptic

No doubt Paul was an apocalyptist during his Pharisaic career. As a Pharisee of the Diaspora, he lived his life in hope of the fulfillment of the messianic promises. Pharisaism was a party, "extremely zealous for the traditions of the fathers" (Gal. 1:14); its "zeal for the law" (Phil. 3:5) expressed itself in its separation from the rest of Judaism, a separation that was linked to the idea of the *Kadoshim* and *Zedakim*, the successors to the "faithful remnant" of Old Testament times, as reformulated in the Maccabean struggle. Paul's zeal for Torah and halakah had been the catalyst for his persecution of the church: "As to zeal a persecutor of the church, as to righteousness under the law blameless" (Phil. 3:6). His theological reason for persecuting the church was evoked by the heretical consequences that Hellenistic-Jewish Christians like the Stephen group drew from their confession of the crucified Jesus as the Messiah. We can be sure that Paul, like Judaism in general, did not consistently persecute the Jerusalem Christians but rather persecuted the Hellenistic-Jewish Christians who gathered, for instance, in Damascus (Acts 9:1), that is, those Christians who had relaxed their observance of the Torah and who, according to Acts 6:11, 13, spoke "against Moses and the temple." These Hellenistic-Jewish Christians had started the Gentile mission (Acts 11:19–26) and had committed a cardinal sin in the eyes of the Pharisees. They had breached the domain of Judaism in allowing Gentiles to participate in the messianic promises without circumcision and without observance of the "whole law" (Gal. 5:3). They regarded Gentiles as Christian proselytes who were admitted to the Christian "way" but without obligation to the whole law.

Paul's apocalyptic conviction was not initiated by his conversion to Christ but formed the background of his Pharisaic world view. The discontinuity between Paul the Pharisee and Paul the Christian lies in a different posture toward the relation between the Torah and the messianic promises and not in a change from "legal casuistic Pharisaism" (Paul the Pharisee) to "universalistic apocalyptic thinking" (Paul the Christian). Because Paul had probably been an apocalyptic Pharisaic "missionary" before his conversion, if we can trust Acts 9:1–2, the apocalyptic structure of his thought remains the constant in his Pharisaic and Christian life.

The truth of this assertion is evident from the Pauline letters, because apocalyptic persists from the earliest letter (1 Thessalonians) to the latest (Philippians). Apocalyptic is not a peripheral curiosity for Paul but the central climate and focus of his thought, as it was for most early Christian thinkers. This has been almost dogmatically denied by New Testament scholarship, notwithstanding the researches of Schweitzer and Bousset.[37] Leonhard Goppelt, for example, argues that typology is the crucial category in Paul and opposes it to apocalyptic;[38] Willi Marxsen claims, "Although we quite often find . . . apocalyptic material in Paul's letters, he himself was not an apocalypticist";[39] and Conzelmann states that Paul's theology is based on nonapocalyptic credal formulations.[40] Even Sanders, who emphasizes the apocalyptic stream in Judaism, can say:

> *Since the conventions of apocalypticism had so little influence*
> *on him, the hypothesis might be put forward that before his*
> *conversion and call Paul was not especially apocalyptically*
> *oriented. This is one more reason for not supposing that Paul*
> *began with a set apocalyptic view and fitted Christ into it.*[41]

Paul's passionate temper and life-style are not the result of a personal idiosyncrasy but are part of his awareness that he is the man of the hour whose mission takes place in the last hours of world history. He knows himself to be the eschatological apostle who spans the times between the resurrection of Christ and the final resurrection of the dead.

Paul's gospel is formulated within the basic components of apocalyptic. To be sure, apocalyptic undergoes a profound modification in Paul, but this does not affect the intensity of its expectation (vs., e.g., Baumgarten[42]). Both modification and intensity are henceforth determined by the Christ-event.

The modification of apocalyptic is evident in the fact that Paul (1) does not employ the traditional apocalyptic terminology of "this age" in conjunction with that of "the age to come"; (2) significantly modifies the traditional apocalyptic view of the escalation of the forces of evil in the end time; and (3) rarely uses the terminology "the kingdom of God" (or "the day of the Lord"), and when he does, it is mainly in traditional contexts.

As to point 1, when we compare Paul's writing to Jewish apocalyptic literature (4 Ezra; Apocalypse of Baruch; Qumran) and to, for example, the apocalyptic section of Ephesians, we notice that he uses little of the traditional apocalyptic terminology. The language of "powers," "rulers," "lordships," "thrones," "world rulers of darkness" (Eph. 6:12; cf. Col. 1:16) is restricted mainly to the apocalyptic sections of 1 Cor. 15:24–28 and Rom. 8:38–39 (cf. 1 Cor. 2:6–9). In fact, Paul does not engage in apocalyptic timetables, descriptions of the architecture of heaven, or accounts of demons and angels. He does not relish the rewards of the blessed or delight in the torture of the wicked (cf. Revelation).

The major apocalyptic forces are, for him, those ontological powers that determine the human situation within the context of God's created order and comprise the "field" of death, sin, the law, and the flesh. Paul does not oppose "this age" to "the coming age" (but cf. Ephesians). The reduction of apocalyptic terminology and the absence of apocalyptic speculation signifies that the Christ-event has strongly modified the dualistic structure of normal apocalyptic thought. Although death is "the last enemy" (1 Cor. 15:26), Paul strongly emphasizes both the openness of the present to the future glory of God and the incursion of the future into the present. No apocalypse ever posits the intimacy of communion in "this age" between God as "Abba" and the believers as his "children" and "sons" (Gal. 4:6; Rom. 8:15). The "age to come" is already present, so that Christians can already rejoice, can already claim "the new creation," and can already live in the power of the Spirit.

As to point 2, the presence of the new age in the old entails a modification of the concept of the escalation of evil in the last times as this is found, for instance, in the Jewish doctrine of the messianic woes.[43] The apocalyptic terminology of the "present age" and the "coming age"[44] is at times present in a different guise.[45] Although Paul adopts the contrast of "the sufferings of the present time" versus "the coming glory" from Jewish apocalyptic (Rom. 8:18), he modifies the doctrine of the messianic woes (*thlipseis*): Christians do not simply "endure" the tribulations of the end time and do not simply "wait" for the end of suffering in God's glorious new age. Christians can already "glory" in sufferings (Rom. 5:2), because God's power manifests itself in the midst of suffering. Suffering signifies a redemptive possibility because it takes its stance in the redemptive cross of Christ and is a token of the extension of God's love in Christ for the redemption of the world (Rom. 8:17–30).

As to point 3, the proleptic presence of the new in the old is probably the reason for Paul's sparing use of the terminology of the kingdom of God (*basileia tou theou*) as the future reality of salvation. And when he uses it, it is in clearly traditional contexts, borrowed from the Jewish-Hellenistic church: "king" (*basileus*; cf. 1 Tim. 1:17; 6:15) and "kingdom" (*basileia*) are not terms that are integral to Paul's thought, although the verb "to reign" (*basileuein*) occupies an important place (Rom. 5:14, 17, 21; 6:12; 1 Cor. 4:8; 15:25). The phrase "kingdom of God" occurs eight times in the authentic letters: Rom. 14:17; 1 Cor. 4:20; 6:9, 10; 15:24, 50; Gal. 5:21; 1 Thess. 2:12. The inclusive view of the age to come as an already operative reality is especially clear in Rom. 14:17: "For the kingdom of God is not food and drink but righteousness and peace and joy in the Holy Spirit." Paul, however, never refers to the kingdom as "the kingdom of Christ" (but cf. Col. 1:13). We can say, then, that traditional apocalyptic thinking in terms of the two ages and their strict temporal dualism is only peripherally present in Paul because the old age has run its course already: "the end of the ages has come" upon us (1 Cor. 10:11; perfect tense, *katēntēken*) and the "fulness of time" has occurred in Christ (Gal. 4:4).[46]

The intensity of Paul's apocalyptic religion is characterized by hope (*elpis*).

> *Through him [Jesus Christ] we have obtained access to this grace in which we stand, and we rejoice in our hope of sharing the glory of God [Rom. 5:2].*

> *For in this hope we were saved. Now hope that is seen is not hope. For who hopes for what he sees? But if we hope for what we do not see, we wait for it with patience [Rom. 8:24, 25].*

> *For they themselves report . . . how you turned to God from idols, to serve a living and true God, and to wait for his Son from heaven, whom he raised from the dead, Jesus who delivers us from the wrath to come [1 Thess. 1:9–10].*

*For we must all appear before the judgment seat of Christ, so that each one may receive good or evil according to what he has done in the body [2 Cor. 5:10].*

Because hope in Paul is not simply a component of faith, Bultmann's characterization of hope as an inherent quality of faith is to be rejected. Hope is, for Bultmann, no longer hope in a specific object.[47] For Paul, hope is not only a believing posture, but something that has a specific content. Abraham epitomizes the hope of the believer: "In hope he believed against hope" (Rom. 4:18). Here hope is a characteristic of faith and identical with the attitude of the Old Testament believer whose faith is simultaneously a hoping in the Lord (cf. especially the Psalms). Faith, hope, and trust are synonyms in the Old Testament (*batah; kawah; amān*) and this meaning persists in Paul and the New Testament.

However, hope has also a specific content and signifies the hoped-for reality. Thus the "waiting" and "patience" that accompany hope, along with the "sighing" of the Christian, have a specific object. Hope is not simply the possibility of an open future or faith in God "who always comes to us from the future"[48] but also the glory of the age to come (Rom. 5:2; 8:18) or the redemption of the body (Rom. 8:23) or the Parousia of Christ (1 Thess. 1:10) or cosmic peace (Rom. 5:1; cf. also Gal. 5:5), that is, the specific blessings of the kingdom of God. Faith not only is hope but it has a hope; it cannot exist without the specific object of the hope.

Paul posits a distinct difference between the promise and the hope and rarely uses the promise for the hope of the Christian or as the content of the Christian hope (except for the probably non-Pauline interpolation of 2 Cor. 6:14–7:1, Paul alludes in Romans 4 to Abraham's faith in the promise as constitutive of Christian faith; see Chapter 6 in my *Paul the Apostle*). The promise refers exclusively to the Old Testament promises, which according to Paul are "confirmed" by Christ (2 Cor. 1:19–20; Rom. 4:16). Thus, the Gentiles have received in Christ the "promised Spirit" (Gal. 3:14; cf. also Gal. 3:22 and Eph. 1:14; *epangelian pneumatos*). The promise and the hope refer to different objects, as the terminological shift from promise (Romans 4) to hope (Romans 5) in Romans shows. Whereas the object of the promise is the Christ-event that is its "confirmation," the object of Christian hope is directed not to the death and resurrection of Christ but rather to those realities of glory that the Christ-event has opened up for the future (Rom. 8:18–30; cf. Col. 1:27, "Christ, the hope of glory"). The hope shares with the promise its specific content, for example, "the redemption of our bodies" (Rom. 8:23) or "an eternal weight of glory" (2 Cor. 4:17; cf. Col. 1:5). Hebrews differs from Paul on this point, because for that author the promise and the hope are fused and both Old and New Testament believers are united in the same "hope" and "promises." Paul's strong christological emphasis makes him differentiate between the promise and the hope: Christ not only "ratifies" the Old Testament "promises" but also opens them up anew as "hope," because in Christ the promises have been given a new basis. In other words, the Old Testament promises are not made obsolete by the Christ-event but are taken up in the hope. Thus, Paul speaks not about the fulfillment of the promises but about their confirmation in Christ (Rom. 4:16, *bebaios*). Indeed, the Christ-event ratifies the Old Testament promises, but it is not a closure event, because it reactivates the hope of his Parousia in glory (1 Cor. 1:7, 8). And it seems that the hope entails the expectation of new revelation and new acts of God. For although the Christ-event as confirmation of the promise and as catalyst of the hope determines the quality of the future hope, the eschatological hope contains the expectation of new acts of God, such as Israel's eschatological conversion or the liberation of creation or the "mystery" of change (1 Cor. 15:50) or the "mystery" of Israel's way of salvation (Rom. 11:25).

In summary, just as "glory" is not only an attribute of the majesty of God but also a dominion and state of glory in the new age (Rom. 8:18), so hope in its relation to glory (Rom. 5:2) is not just the posture of faith but is directed toward a specific object, time, and place: the time and place of the Parousia and the glory to come.

Faith, like hope, has for Paul a specific object. Faith is "saving faith," because Christ is its object and content; it has no inherent virtue in and of itself. The gospel is not distinct from the law because it celebrates "simple trust" or inarticulate "goodwill" instead of "works" and a search for "merits." Judaism, of course, also knows the reality of faith and mercy, so that a faith/works antithesis in this simplistic form would not have served Paul at all in his polemic with Judaism. In Paul as in Luther, *sola fide* is inseparable from *solus Christus*. Faith, to be sure, has a variety of connotations. It can mean assent, obedience, trust, commitment, or the message of faith (cf. *akoē*, Gal. 3:5; Rom. 10:16). It often occurs within a setting of endurance (*hypomonē*), patience (*makrothymia*), and waiting (*apodechomai*), that is, within a context of the practice of hope (cf. Rom. 5:3–5; 8:25; especially 1 Thess. 1:3: "Remembering before our God and Father your work of faith and labor of love and steadfastness of hope in our Lord Jesus Christ"; Gal. 5:5: "For through the Spirit, by faith, we wait for the hope of righteousness"). Just as "the Spirit" is the drawing power of the future "glory" in the present, so "faith" is the power of "salvation" (*sōtēria*) in the present, and makes us eagerly wait for its future realization (Rom. 5:1–11; 4:20–25). Faith motivates our endurance because it is the first installment of that future salvation that we now possess in Christ as righteousness (Rom. 5:9–11). "We walk by faith, not by sight," says Paul (2 Cor. 5:7), but that means that faith itself waits for the consummation of sight. "For now we see in a mirror dimly, but then face to face" (1 Cor. 13:12). Thus, faith relates to hope in the way that righteousness relates to salvation, and "faith-righteousness" (Rom. 4:13) is inseparable from that righteousness or salvation that is our eschatological destiny (Gal. 5:5).

In Paul hope has an apocalyptic specificity. It centers on a happening in time and space that is the object of the yearning and sighing of the Christian, that is, the victory over evil and death in the

Parousia of Christ or the kingdom of God (1 Cor. 15:24). Paul's apocalyptic dualism is not a Gnostic dualism of contempt for this world,
or otherworldliness. It is determined by the event of Christ, an event
that not only negated the old order but also initiated the hope for the
transformation of the creation that has gone astray and is in travail
because it longs for its redemption from decay (Rom. 8:20). Although
the glory of God will break into our fallen world, it will not annihi-
late the world but only break off its present structure of death, because
it aims to transform the cosmos rather than to confirm its ontological
nothingness.

The resurrection of Christ marks the beginning of the process
of transformation, and its historical reality is therefore crucial to Paul
because it marks the appearance of the end in history and not simply
the end of history. It is not an intrapsychic event; rather, it appeals
to the Christian's solidarity with the stuff of creation that God has
destined for "resurrection" glory.

### Critical Evaluation

A final observation: Paul's modification of apocalyptic should not be
exaggerated or be construed in terms of an abstruse dialectic. Jürgen
Becker and Heinz-Wolfgang Kuhn have pointed out that the distinction between primitive Christianity and Judaism does not lie simply in
their different conceptions of salvation, with one viewing it as present
reality and the other as a purely future hope. Qumran has demonstrated clearly that the new age is already appropriated as a present
reality and is not simply a future expectation. The community knows
itself to be the new temple and the new covenant and celebrates the
Spirit in its midst.[49] This means that the difference between at least
a form of apocalyptic Judaism and Pauline Christianity must not be
drawn in terms of temporal distinctions. Rather it raises the question
about the mode and quality of the new in the present. And as we shall
see, the issue of the Torah will turn out to be the decisive difference in
the Jewish and Christian understandings of the quality of the new age.

Moreover, the presence of the new in the old is often interpreted in terms of the distinction "presently hidden" versus "publicly revealed in the kingdom of God."[50] This interpretation can certainly draw on Paul inasmuch as he opposes "faith" to "sight" (2 Cor. 5:5), speaks—although rarely—about "revelation" (*apokalypsis*) as a future phenomenon (1 Cor. 1:7; Rom. 8:19; but Gal. 1:12), and views the Christ-event as a proleptic anticipation of God's final glory. However, the Lutheran emphases on the word of God and faith as revelation of the hidden God (*deus abscon-ditus*) constitute too narrow an interpretation of Paul's view of the reality of the new age in the present. Because the Catholic interpretation of "the new creation" in Christ as a sacramental reality *ex opere operato* errs in the opposite direction, and because Paul cannot be drawn into a scheme of "realized eschatology," the precise interpretation of the presence of the new in the old is still a hotly debated issue (see Chapters 11 and 12 in my *Paul the Apostle*). At this point, two observations are in order.

The interpretation of the new in the old in terms of "hidden" versus "public" imposes upon Paul a dualism between the old and the new that seems unwarranted. The history of Israel is for Paul not simply the old age of darkness;[51] he softens the dualism between the ages by interpreting Israel's history in a typological light. Thus, the past is not just the age of sin and death but also the era of God's salvation-historical imprint. The era of "the old covenant" has its own (temporary) "splendor" (2 Cor. 3:7–11); the Exodus story has eschatological meaning for believers (1 Cor. 10:1–13); the privileges of Israel are real and abiding (Romans 9–11), and although Christ is the end of the law (Rom. 10:4), the law is "holy and righteous and good" and plays a necessary part in salvation-history (see Chapter 11 in my *Paul the Apostle*). The past contains the footprints of the promises of God, and these promises are taken up into the new rather than cast aside. Therefore, if the past of the old age already contains the hidden presence of God's promises, then the presence of God's act in Christ is not simply a hidden presence: "Therefore, if any one is in Christ, he is a new creation" (2 Cor. 5:17). This issue is crucial for Paul because God's righteousness and his faithfulness to his promises to Israel are at stake. Romans demonstrates that the question of God's faithfulness to Israel is answered in the gospel, and the affirmation of God's faithfulness demonstrates in turn the reliability of God's act in Christ for the salvation of the Gentiles.

The "hidden"/"public" scheme rests on an interpretation of Paul that views him in combat with Gnostic religious convictions. Thus, Paul stresses the utter dependence of the believer on the word of God, who justifies the ungodly by faith alone, instead of the sacramental realism of proto-gnosticism or Gnostic religion. The believer is the *simul justus et peccator* who lives by faith in the "nude" promise of God, and so Christian visibility in the world tends to be exclusively defined in terms of "weakness" that is made perfect by the grace of God alone (2 Cor. 12:9–10). This construal is promoted by the Lutheran emphasis on faith in the word of God and on the correlation of *sola fide* and *solus Christus* that corresponds to Paul's view.

However, the interpretation of Paul in terms of a Gnostic combat situation has been eroded by the Nag Hammadi evidence, because it has become increasingly difficult to detect a coherent Gnostic system in the pages of the New Testament. Moreover, the resurrection of Christ has a clear historical-ontological referent in Paul; it is attested to by witnesses (1 Cor. 15:6) and is therefore not just a "kerygmatic" event. Indeed, the resurrection of Christ releases the Spirit, which manifests itself concretely in "signs, wonders and mighty works" (2 Cor. 12:12; Rom. 15:18–19) and in glossolalia, prophecy, and healings (1 Corinthians 12–14). Moreover, the believer is "a new creation" in Christ (2 Cor. 5:17; Gal. 6:15) and participates in the life of Christ in such a way that his Christian status is visible in the world; nonbelievers confess to the presence of Christ in the church (1 Cor. 14:25) and believers can resist the "deeds of the body" (Rom. 8:13) and can live like "shining lights in the world" (Phil. 3:15). In this light, unqualified speech about the "incognito life" of Christians or about the "hidden" character of life in Christ is clearly insufficient. The contextual situation determines for Paul his particular theological pitch (see Chapter 12 in my *Paul the Apostle*), and his response to enthusiasts is quite different from his response to Judaizers and Jews. It is clear, however, that Paul integrates the categories of justification by faith and those of participation in Christ. Therefore, the antithesis "hidden"/"revealed" is too one-sided because it imposes upon Paul's christological modification of apocalyptic a dualistic scheme that characterizes more the old age of darkness and the invisibility of faith than the new age that detects the coming dawn of God's glory on the horizon of the world. The radical difference between the old and the new is no longer the same as in apocalyptic Judaism, and it is not to be interpreted exclusively in terms of the dialectic of the hidden presence of the new within the old. The Christ-event makes it possible for Paul to speak about the proleptic new in the present that is ushering in the full glory of God.

## The Resurrection of Christ and the Future Resurrection of the Dead

### The Resurrection of Christ as Apocalyptic Event

We must remember that the resurrection of Christ heightened rather than relaxed the longing for the Parousia.

> *For they themselves report concerning us what a welcome we had among you, and how you turned to God from idols, to serve a living and true God, and to wait for his Son from heaven, whom he raised from the dead, Jesus who delivers us from the wrath to come [1 Thess. 1:9–10].*

> *But our commonwealth is in heaven, and from it we await a Savior, the Lord Jesus Christ, who will change our lowly body to be like his glorious body, by the power which enables him even to subject all things to himself [Phil. 3:20–21; cf. 1 Cor. 15:20–28].*

Resurrection language is end-time language and unintelligible apart from the apocalyptic thought world to which resurrection language belongs. Resurrection language properly belongs to the domain of the new age to come and is an inherent part of the transformation and the recreation of all reality in the apocalyptic age. Thus, the resurrection of Christ, the coming reign of God, and the future resurrection of the dead belong together. The new creation in Christ (*kainē ktisis*, 2 Cor. 5:17; Gal. 6:15) is an anticipation of the final resurrection of the dead and a new act of creation by the God who "raises the dead and who calls into existence the things that do not exist" (Rom. 4:17). "Resurrection," then, has not just ideational significance, as if it marks a new perception of things (resurrection as language, or kerygmatic, event); it also has a clear historical and ontological reference because it addresses itself to the transformation of the created order. Therefore, the resurrection of Jesus is not simply synonymous with a heavenly "translation," "assumption" (Enoch, Elijah), "ascension" or "rebirth" (cf. the mystery religions). Paul does not think of Jesus' ascension in terms of a removal scene, as if a Gnostic savior figure leaves the scene of corrupted matter by shedding his body on the cross and by ascending to his proper heavenly abode, where Spirit conjoins Spirit. Neither is Jesus' resurrection a "historical reunion scene," as if Jesus returns to the flesh and continues in some sense his earlier companionship with his disciples, eating with them, talking with them, and so on (Luke 24). We must not forget that empty-tomb traditions do not play any role in Paul's thought. "He was buried" (*etaphē*, 1 Cor. 15:4) underscores the reality of the death of Christ. The resurrection of Christ means primarily the "bodily" exaltation of Christ by God and his enthronement to his heavenly lordship (Phil. 2:11). It signifies the exaltation of the crucified Christ, that is, it is a proleptic event that foreshadows the apocalyptic general resurrection of the dead and thus the transformation of our created world and the gift of new corporeal life to dead bodies. Resurrection is a historical-ontological category, manifesting in this world the dawning of the new age of transformation.

Thus, the God "who gives life to the dead" (Rom. 4:17; 2 Cor. 1:9) is not so much the God of miraculous intervention in general but specifically the God who since the resurrection of Christ has initiated the resurrection world as the creator-redeemer, who "calls into existence the things that do not exist" (Rom. 4:17). Resurrection language expresses the new age in the midst of the old: Paul stresses the resurrection of the body, not the resurrection of the flesh.[52] A resurrection of the flesh signals a loss of Paul's apocalyptic thinking; it underscores the continuity between the old age and the new age to such an extent that the spiritual transformation of the new age is ignored.

The final resurrection is total renewal in an apocalyptic sense: "the new world" (*palingenesia*, Matt. 19:28; 1 Clem. 9:4; cf. Mark 12:23: "In the resurrection [*anastasis*] whose wife will she be?"). And so Paul can call Israel's conversion in the eschatological age "life from the dead" (Rom. 11:15). Because resurrection is an apocalyptic category, the resurrection of Christ can only be understood apocalyptically as the preliminary manifestation of the general resurrection in the age to come. Therefore, Paul characterizes the risen Christ as "the first fruits of those who have fallen asleep" (1 Cor. 15:20) or as "the first-born among many brethren" (Rom. 8:29; cf. Col. 1:16), so that the resurrection of Christ announces the imminent dawn of the general resurrection to come.

## The Resurrection of Christ as Isolated Event

We must be aware of the fact that resurrection language cannot function properly when it is divorced from this temporal and cosmological framework, because there is a necessary correlation between the resurrection of Christ and the age to come. If we divorce the two events by allocating the age to come to a far-off point, or if we retain one event and discard the other by eliminating the age to come as myth and by retaining the resurrection of Christ as in some sense a historical event, resurrection language is forced to function in a new semantic field, where it loses its intended meaning. In a Gnostic setting, resurrection of the dead becomes a heavenly ascent of the pneumatic self, shedding the material body in order to be absorbed in the unity of the Pleroma. In later Catholic Christianity, it becomes synonymous with the immortality of the individual soul after death, a development that was foreshadowed in Hellenistic Judaism, which conceived of the resurrection in an immaterial way, that is, as the ascension of the soul to heaven (Wisdom of Solomon; 2 and 4 Maccabees). However, when the resurrection of Christ is divorced from the new age to come (cf. Bultmann), its cosmological aspect is not only individualized and spiritualized but its temporal aspect is also reduced to a "postmortem" immortality of the soul. Even when interpreters unmask the Greek anthropology of a dualism between spirit and body as nonbiblical and reject the doctrine of the immortality of the soul, the failure to acknowledge Paul's apocalyptic eschatology as the carrier of his thought undermines the significance of the resurrection for Paul and so misconstrues Paul's thought as a whole. As I noted earlier, Neoorthodoxy in all its forms collapses apocalypticism into Christology. Bultmann defines Paul's eschatology as the "now" of God's salvation in Christ and rejects his apocalypticism as a survival.[53] Eschatology becomes the possibility for genuine human authenticity due to the word of Christ in the gospel, and the resurrection of Christ is reduced to an intrapsychic event or to an existentialist event, that is, to a new self-understanding in the world. It becomes the perception of the meaning of the cross and thus loses both its character as event and its temporal apocalyptic mooring. The resurrection event is thus isolated from its apocalyptic setting with the assistance of an interpretation of myth that centers on the historicity of man.[54] If anthropology becomes the sole criterion for Pauline theology, the resurrection no longer has an ontological-cosmological meaning and instead is conflated exclusively with the realm of human decision and possibility.

The collapse of apocalypticism into Christology or anthropology causes a disorientation of Paul's proclamation of the resurrection, which has grave consequences for Paul's thought. Individualism and spiritualization—if not ecclesiastical self-aggrandizement—are the inevitable results of such an interpretation. Moreover, the neglect of the cosmic-temporal elements of Paul's apocalyptic thought leads to a neglect of his "ecological" and cosmic themes and so to a misconstrual of both his anthropology and ecclesiology, for the somatic worldly component of that anthropology cannot be spiritualized away—as Käsemann correctly observes.[55] Paul's church is not an aggregate of justified sinners or a sacramental institute or a means for private self-sanctification but the avant-garde of the new creation in a hostile world, creating beachheads in this world of God's dawning new world and yearning for the day of God's visible lordship over his creation, the general resurrection of the dead (see Chapter 14 in my *Paul the Apostle*).

The relation between apocalyptic cosmology and anthropology is, to be sure, crucial in Paul. Bultmann has underscored Paul's anthropological focus in his *New Testament Theology*. Pauline theology is discussed there under the themes "Man [*der Mensch*] prior to the revelation of faith" and "Man [*der Mensch*] under faith."[56] After a discussion of Paul's anthropological concepts and the forces that imprison man ("flesh, sin, world and the law"), the theme is explicated under the concept "righteousness," which Bultmann understands in Lutheran fashion to be a divine gift to man.[57] Throughout the discussion the cosmological-ontological aspects of Paul's thought are subjected to an existentialist interpretation. The themes of the person in solidarity with the created order; the resurrection as a distinct historical event and as inaugurating the final resurrection of the dead; the world (*kosmos*) as the created order that involves more than "humankind"—all are neglected or demythologized. Notwithstanding the crucial importance of anthropology for Paul and his rejection of apocalyptic speculation, anthropology becomes disoriented if it is not viewed within the coordinates of the "objective" categories of the Christ-event and of the created order. The resurrection of Christ and the final resurrection of the dead are crucial events, not because they are the guarantee of eternal personal survival but because they express the inner connection of the salvation of the created order with the final triumph of God. For the resurrection of the dead signals the liberation of the created order "to the freedom of the glory of the children of God" (Rom. 8:21; trans. mine).

When the resurrection of Christ is isolated from its linguistic apocalyptic environment and from the reality of future apocalyptic renewal, it may well retain its traditional nomenclature in expositions of Paul's thought, but it becomes something radically different. It becomes actually a docetic miracle in the midst of history without affecting the historical process itself, that is, an event in the midst of history rather than at the end of history for the sake of history's transformation. Attention now shifts to the resurrection as the end of the incarnation, as a closure event rather than as an inaugural event. This happens, for instance, in John, where—notwithstanding 16:13 ("the Spirit will declare to you the things that are to come")—future eschatology is absorbed by the resurrection of Christ and the gift of the Spirit. Given John's Christocentric emphasis, the future becomes purely an unfolding of what has happened once for all in the Christ-event. Thus, the resurrection completes the itinerary of the Son of God from pre- to postexistence and simply confirms the truth of the incarnation. The identity between the Jesus of history and the risen Christ is asserted in such a way that the risen Christ is portrayed as "divinity in the flesh" on earth (John 20:20, 24–29; 21:4–8; Matt. 28:9; Luke 24:38–43). Such a portrayal necessitates logically an ascension, separable from the resurrection and the forty days of Jesus' postresurrection stay on earth with his disciples (Acts 1). From now on, empty-tomb traditions are used to stress Christ's divine character on earth after his resurrection or to show the divine continuum between Jesus' pre- and postresurrection life. In John, for instance, Jesus' historical life seems to be a theophany of a deity in "rabbinic clothes," because the distinction between the historical and resurrection life of Jesus becomes blurred.[58] The resurrection of Christ is interpreted as the exaltation of Christ, that is, as his present lordship in heaven and his present activity in the

Spirit, but in such a way that it is no longer connected with the imminent resurrection of the dead and the cosmic renewal of creation. Even in the synoptic Gospels (especially Matt. 28:18) the present "authority" (*exousia*) of the risen Lord seems more important than his Parousia at "the close of the age" (Matt. 28:20, *synteleia tou aiōnos*), and none of the Synoptics makes any reference in its resurrection stories to Christ as the "first born" of the dead or to the final resurrection of the dead (but cf. Matt. 27:52–53). The conception of resurrection as exaltation without an inherent connection with the final resurrection and God's imminent apocalyptic triumph leads to the problem of Hellenistic Christianity (cf. 1 Corinthians 15). For Paul, resurrection as exaltation is the first stage toward the resurrection of the dead, whereas for the Corinthians the exaltation of Christ simply means the completed eschatological glory of Christ. Thus, exaltation Christology is capable of minimizing the final resurrection of the dead. Death is no longer the last enemy to be overcome (1 Cor. 15:26), it has been overcome (cf. 2 Tim. 1:10; 2:18); the final resurrection has already occurred in—and with—the resurrection of Christ. In a Gnostic environment, stories and sayings like Luke 16:19–31 and 23:32 (cf. Luke 23:46; Ps. 31:6) are interpreted as "realized eschatology." Chrysostom reports that the Manichaeans interpret Luke 23:43, "Truly, I say to you, today you will be with me in Paradise," as the full presence of salvation in the present, which according to them makes a resurrection of the dead superfluous. The heretics of 2 Tim. 2:18 may have had similar thoughts.[59] Furthermore, an exaltation Christology allows a dualistic interpretation and a denial of a "resurrection body": Hippolytus tells us that Justin, the Gnostic, taught that Jesus' body remained on the cross, whereas his pure Spirit went to the Father.[60]

Along these lines, the resurrection, with its apocalyptic coordinates of the general resurrection and the imminence of the Parousia, was reinterpreted nonapocalyptically in the postapostolic era.

(1) The resurrection interprets Jesus' life as a closure event, that is, as the final confirmation of the divine status of Jesus in his incarnate life. And so the "life of Jesus" becomes a "foundation story" that occupies the position of the "center of history" and loses its firm connection with the coming kingdom of God and the final resurrection of the dead (cf. already Luke).

(2) It stresses in antidocetic fashion the reality of Jesus as the Christ and thus centers more on the identity of Jesus as the eternal Son of God than on Jesus as the inaugurator of the final resurrection and the kingdom of God.

(3) It confirms the divine preexistence of Christ and his incarnation and so construes an analogy between the incarnation and the resurrection: Just as the postresurrection Jesus is divinity in the flesh, so the incarnate Jesus is divinity in the flesh.

(4) The resurrection signifies the exaltation of Christ, whose grace is available through the sacraments of the church, "the kingdom of Christ," and whose reign can now be located in the hierarchical offices of the church.

(5) The resurrection of the dead becomes an individualistic postmortem immortality and an individualistic "last" judgment.

(6) The cosmic resurrection of the dead and the future kingdom of God become a far-off proper "conclusion" to the created order. They function, as it were, as the proper end for systematic doctrinal thought: Just as our transient creation has a beginning, it has an end in the eternal being of God, so that both "beginning" and "end" are embraced by the timelessness and eternity of God.

We conclude that the intrusion of Hellenistic categories in the history of doctrine has pushed aside the apocalyptic coordinates of the resurrection of Christ and the final resurrection of the dead, with the result that the triumph of God through Christ has become solely the triumph of Christ over our personal death, and the kingdom of Christ as present in the church has displaced the expectation of the coming triumph of God over his creation.

Indeed, increasingly in the history of the early church, the resurrection of Christ propels the question of his preexistence. Although Paul himself relates the resurrection to Christ's preexistence, his focus is not on Christ's preexistence but on his resurrection as the open horizon for the apocalyptic future.

However, the delay of the Parousia, the shifting philosophical and cultural climate, and the new apologetic missionary demands of the church contributed to a slackening interest in apocalyptic matters; protological rather than eschatological categories became the central concern (cf. the Greek quest for the *archē*). This movement climaxes—via the logos-doctrine of the apologists—in the Nicene struggles and subsequently at Chalcedon. The interest shifts from the resurrection status and imminent return of the Son of God at the right hand of God to the relation between the Father and the Son in preexistence. The development of the logos-theology furthered this tendency, as can be seen in the prologue of John and subsequently in the logos-theology of the apologists. Reflection on God's action "in the end" is displaced by that on God's action "in the beginning." However, the logos speculation contained a twofold danger: (1) a docetic interpretation of the incarnation; (2) a view of the resurrection as a confirmation of the eternal status of the Son of God rather than as the inaugural event of the Parousia. The movement from the resurrection to the incarnation could borrow from Jewish-Hellenistic ontological wisdom categories that were now applied to the Christ-event (cf. Col. 1:15, 18, where "first-born" [*prōtotokos*] as reference to the resurrection of Christ shifts toward "first-born" [*prōtotokos*] as Christ's mediating function in creation [1:15]). Similarly, the meaning of "Parousia" changes. Whereas it is always applied to the future "coming" of Christ in the New Testament, it now refers not to the "second coming" but to the incarnation as the "first coming" (Ignatius; Justin Martyr).

Moreover, because the resurrection of Christ is conceived as a divine miracle within the ongoing historical process and has no basic meaning for the redemption of the created order, it becomes, with the incarnation, the metaphysical junction of matter and spirit, that is, the place where the heavenly world touches the material sphere. The non-Pauline resurrection of the flesh of Christ (cf. Tertullian), that is, of his divine "materialization" on earth, no longer has a forward-eschatological look that views Christ as "the first in a series to come"; instead, it has a backward look, in order to prove the reality of the incarnation.

## The Bifocal Character of the Resurrection

For Paul, the historicity of the resurrection of Christ and its "bodily" character are crucial. The historicity of the resurrection signifies its eschatological-temporal significance, that is, it is a proleptic event that inaugurates the new creation. The "bodily" character of the resurrection manifests the resurrection as an event that not only occurs in time but also signals the "bodily" ontological transformation of the created order in the kingdom of God. Therefore, the resurrection of Christ is both crucial and yet provisional. It is crucial because it marks the beginning of the new creation; it is provisional because it looks forward to the consummation of that beginning. The resurrection of Christ thus underscores two interrelated features of Paul's thought: the abiding significance of the apocalyptic framework, and the Christ-event as both crucial and yet provisional.

The resurrection of Christ heightens the tension in the Jewish-apocalyptic scheme of the two ages between the "already" and "not yet." Contrary to widespread opinion (cf., e.g., Cullmann), this tension is not unique to the gospel because Jewish apocalyptic circles like Qumran exhibit a similar tension. The Qumran community knows itself to be alive in the end time and to be "the new covenant" of the saved, in possession of the eschatological Spirit,[61] so that it already claims the gifts of the end time in its midst. Therefore, it is not the tension itself, but the interpretation of its particular quality, that must be explored in Paul. Although the new age has already dawned with the resurrection of Christ, and although faith in Christ means a life of eschatological peace with God (Rom. 5:1), the "already" is not to be fused with the "not yet." The time of the consummation or the Parousia of Christ is "not yet," and "sight" has "not yet" displaced "faith" (2 Cor. 5:5). Cullmann introduces the analogy of D-Day and V-Day of World War II to illustrate this tension.[62] A. M. Hunter describes it as follows:

> But Paul's gospel like that of the whole New Testament was set in a framework of both realized and futurist eschatology. D-Day was but the prelude to V-Day, the Day of Christ, the parousia, the day of the final victory of God in Christ. It is the conviction that though the campaign may drag on and V-Day, the day of final glory may still be out of sight, D-Day is over and the powers of evil have received a blow from which they can never recover.[63]

Paul's thought, then, is bifocal. With the Christ-event, history has become an ellipse with two foci: the Christ-event and the Parousia, or the day of God's final victory. The dynamic tension between the two foci characterizes Paul's thought. He considers the Parousia to be imminent and his apostolic mission to be the preparation for its coming. Therefore, its success will be his eschatological reward on the day of the last judgment (1 Thess. 2:20; Phil. 2:16; 4:1) and its possible failure a reason for his exclusion from eternal life (1 Cor. 9:24–27; 1 Thess. 2:19). "We shall not all sleep, but we shall all be changed" (1 Cor. 15:51; cf. 1 Thess. 4:13; 5:23). And even where this confidence is shaken by the perilous events of his life (2 Cor. 1:9; Phil. 1:19–26; 2:17), the hope persists that "not much time is left" (1 Cor. 7:29) and that the true "commonwealth" of the Christian is in heaven, from where Christ will imminently return (Phil. 3:20–21).

## The Transposition of the Apocalyptic Framework

However, although this dynamic tension is the lifeblood of Paul's escha-tological self-understanding, Christian religious life is unable to main-tain its fervent longing for the end time. An atmosphere may prevail in which the Jewish apocalyptic world view—with its passion for the public manifestation of God's final righteousness and victory—ceases to be the focal concern. In such a situation, the apocalyptic framework is being discarded and transposed into something else. The tension of the gospel, inherent in the interaction of the two foci of the Christ-event and the final glory of God, snaps and collapses. In the course of church history the tendency has been to stress one of the foci over the other, so that either the "already" or the "not yet" receives almost exclu-sive attention. Sometimes—as in apocalyptic sectarianism—a purely apocalyptic outlook reestablishes itself and minimizes the "already" of God's action in Christ. Yet the prevailing option in the history of Christian thought collapses the "not yet" into the "already," so that the eschatological future becomes purely a "doctrine about the last things" (*doctrina de novissimis*), like purgatory, the interim state of the dead, and the far-off conclusion of God's dealing with the created world.

In the New Testament we notice this movement away from the temporal tension inherent in Paul's apocalyptic theology. Two solutions seem to present themselves: (1) a diffusion of the tension between the foci, or (2) a conflation of the foci. The first solution postpones the apocalyptic hour (cf. esp. 2 Peter, 2 Thessalonians, Luke-Acts); the second solution spiritualizes it (cf. esp. Colossians, Ephesians, John).

Second Peter alters the conception of time from historical chronology into a divine conception of time, in order to come to terms with the delay of the Parousia. The question of the heretics is, "Where is the promise of his coming? For ever since the fathers fell asleep, all things have continued as they were from the beginning of creation" (3:4). And Peter answers, "Do not ignore this one fact, beloved, that with the Lord one day is as a thousand years, and a thousand years as one day" (3:8).

Although we may appreciate Peter's attempt to retain the apocalyptic Parousia (2 Pet. 3:8–14), his attempted solution is a peculiar mixture of the Stoic-philosophical doctrine of the end of the world ("conflagration," *ekpurōsis*; cf. 2 Pet. 3:7, 10) and the traditional Christian teaching of the "day of the Lord" coming "like a thief" (3:10). Peter changes chronological time into a scheme that, although not timeless, is no longer able to address the early Christian urgency of time. He postpones the Parousia for the sake of the repentance of all (3:9). The tone has changed. The imminence of the Parousia does not motivate man's urgent need for repentance (as, e.g., in Heb. 6:4–8; 9:27–28); rather, man's need for repentance makes the delay of the Parousia necessary (cf. the "second chance" to repent in Hermas).

In a similar way, 2 Thessalonians snaps the tension between the two foci when the author inserts a specific apocalyptic program between the present and the Parousia (2 Thess. 2:1–12). He intends to retain the emphasis on the future age, especially because he struggles against an enthusiastic spiritualism that knows itself to be participating already in the kingdom of God. "Now concerning the coming of our Lord Jesus Christ and our assembling to meet him, we beg you, brethren, not to be quickly shaken in mind or excited, either by spirit or by word, or by letter purporting to be from us, to the effect that the day of the Lord has come" (2 Thess. 2:1–2).[64] The author—unlike Paul—defines in his apocalyptic program the impending future as the time of the messianic woes. The future is not the time of the Parousia but the time of the messianic woes that precede the Parousia (cf. "first," *prōton* [2 Thess. 2:3] vs. "then," *tote* [v. 8]). The apocalyptic time of the Antichrist is not yet; it is "held up" (v. 7) by a mysterious "restrainer," probably the apostle Paul himself in his missionary career. Although the author characterizes the present time as a time of affliction (*thlipseis*; *diōgmoi*; 2 Thess. 1:4), the present "tribulation" (*thlipseis*) will be followed by a time of extreme crisis, "the rebellion" (*apostasia*, 2:3) before the Parousia. In other words, more "tribulations" are to come. The author argues for a delay of the Parousia with the help of an apocalyptic timetable. Unlike Paul, he is unable to stress the immi-nence of the Parousia and to resist enthusiasm (cf. 1 Corinthians). Paul relates the two foci—Christ and the Parousia—in such a way that he is able to maintain both the presence of salvation and its future consummation. Second Thessalonians, to the contrary, responds to a spiritualistic interpretation of the kingdom with a postponement of the Parousia and a need for endurance. The balance between Christ and the Parousia is here surrendered for the sake of an apocalyptic pro-gram, with the result that the tension between the two foci of Christ and the Parousia is no longer maintained in its integrity.

The writer of Luke-Acts is a master theologian who is not, like the authors of 2 Peter and 2 Thessalonians, satisfied with a simple correction of the problem of the delay of the Parousia. Instead, he restructures the relation between the two foci and places the Christ-event at "the center of time" (Conzelmann). His salvation-historical sketch turns attention away from the problem of the delay of the Parousia. What occupies him is the present time as a time of missions. Although he does not deny the Parousia and its expectation (Acts 1:11; 3:20–21), he allows it to fade away to the periphery (cf. his use of *basileia* = preaching the gospel: Acts 8:12; 19:8; 20:25; 28:31). Luke aptly uses the solution of apocalyptic postponement to concentrate on the missionary demands of the church. The temporal end of time is diffused for the sake of the mission of the church. It is displaced, as it were, by the geographical end of the mission to the ends of the earth (Acts 1:1–8), that is, to Rome as the center of the Roman Empire (Acts 28).[65]

At the other end of the spectrum, the apocalyptic future is not postponed but conflated with the Christ-event. Here the "not yet" focus disappears in favor of the "already." Present and future are not stretched apart but collapse into each other. The author of 2 Tim. 2:18–19, for example, indicts the opponents of Paul in the following way: "Among them are Hymenaeus and Philetus, who have swerved from the truth by holding that the resurrection is past already. They are upsetting the faith of some." Indeed, it was easy to misunderstand

Paul's preaching of the Christ-event in this manner, given the enthusiastic atmosphere of the early church with its abundance of Spirit-gifts and prophetic inspirations, especially when we remember the psychological impact that the sociological atmosphere of conflict must have had on the early churches. Eschatological and charismatic phenomena readily abound in sectarian groups that are alienated from the society at large and subjected to its hostility.

When Paul writes, "Behold, now is the acceptable time; behold, now is the day of salvation" (2 Cor. 6:2) or, "Therefore, if any one is in Christ, he is a new creation; the old has passed away, behold, the new has come" (2 Cor. 5:17), the focus of "the already" certainly seems to blot out the "not yet." The demand of the moment within the context of a particular argument can easily lead to a noncontextual hearing of Paul's total message. In 2 Cor. 5:17, for instance, the stress on "the already" appears in a setting that combats adversaries who claim to have esoteric, "sarkic" knowledge of the historical Jesus. In that context the new being of the believer in Christ makes a purely historical knowing of Jesus, that is, a knowing "according to the flesh," irrelevant, because it ignores the eschatological shift that Christ has initiated. However, this contextual argument is easily distorted into "realized eschatology" when it is read apart from its total context. The relation of "the parts to the whole" is a major hermeneutical problem, especially in an author who is engaged in contingent argumentation. When people interpret Paul on the basis of isolated proof texts, which are taken out of the "whole" of his message, Paul is open to misinterpretation.

Elaine Hiesey Pagels has shown how the Valentinian Gnostics could claim Paul as their ally with this proof-text method.[66] It is quite probable that the "selective hearing" of the Corinthians tripped up their interpretation of Paul's gospel and so distorted it enthusiastically in a Gnostic sense. When in a Hellenistic atmosphere the apocalyptic world view is no longer operative, Paul's so-called "eschatological reservation" can be discarded. When in Colossians and Ephesians baptism signifies that Christians have not only been buried with Christ but have also been raised with Christ in the heavenly places (Col. 2:12; 3:1; Eph. 2:4–6), the apocalyptic future collapses into the Christ-event. In this context the church becomes identified with Christ, becoming a heavenly entity and threatening to displace the apocalyptic future. Whereas Rom. 6:1–11 limits our present identification with Christ to our participation in his death, Colossians and Ephesians extend it to our participation in his resurrection as well. When participation in Christ is viewed as a completed state, Christian ethical life is distorted, because it leads to premature spiritual perfection and to a sectarian segregation from the rest of God's creation.

## 1 Corinthians 15 and the Resurrection

Paul's argument in 1 Corinthians 15 demonstrates the importance of his apocalyptic theology. In his argument with people who have a nonapocalyptic, Hellenistic world view, Paul insists on its crucial importance for the truth of the gospel.

### Context

We must first of all determine the place of 1 Corinthians 15 in the context of the whole letter, because 1 Corinthians clearly shows the precarious relation of contingency and coherent center in Paul's thought. In fact, the letter seems to consist of a series of contingent arguments. Contingency is apparent in the multiple concerns to which the letter replies and in the basic shift of the argument, once we move from chapters 1 and 2 to chapter 15. The basic core of the argument appears to center on the death of Christ in chapters 1 and 2 and on the resurrection of Christ in chapter 15. Paul seems, as it were, to divorce the death and resurrection of Christ in 1 Corinthians, because the absence of the resurrection in chapters 1 and 2 is as striking as the absence of the death of Christ in chapter 15. First Corinthians consists primarily of answers to a variety of questions and concerns that had reached Paul by letter and by personal report (1 Cor. 1:11: Chloe; 16:17: Stephanas, Fortunatus, Achaicus). Paul replies to the letter of the Corinthians in

1 Cor. 7:1—16:12 (cf. the "concerning" [*peri*] clauses), whereas he reacts in chapters 1–6 to oral reports (1:11; 5:1). This question-and-answer letter deals with a wide variety of questions: a case of incest, judicial matters, matters of worship, gnosis, marriage, church unity, spiritual gifts, and instructions about the collection. Where in all this variety is unity to be found? What is in fact the "canon in the canon" of the letter? Karl Barth has attempted to demonstrate its underlying consistency by arguing that the contingent questions are held together by the resurrection chapter (chapter 15), which he feels constitutes the climax of the letter.[67] The argument about the resurrection of the dead, then, is not an ad hoc polemical or pastoral concern of Paul but the hidden key to the whole Epistle. Barth's thesis seems to be confirmed by the preface (1 Cor. 1:4–9), because it epitomizes the content of the letter and especially emphasizes the "waiting for the revealing of our Lord Jesus Christ" (1:7) and "his sustenance to the end" (1:8), a theme that is richly developed in chapter 15 (cf. the summary of the content of the letter in vv. 4–9: "speech" [1:5—chapters 1–4]; "gnosis" [1:5—chapters 8–10]; "spiritual gift" [1:7—chapters 12–14]; "waiting for the revelation" [1:7—chapter 15]).[68]

### The Theology of the Corinthians

The Corinthians do not live in an apocalyptic climate; they inhabit the world of Hellenistic cosmology that—though in some ways amenable to an apocalyptic mentality with its dualistic, world-despairing self-understanding—thinks in spatial-vertical categories rather than in the temporal-historical categories of apocalyptic thought. Human destiny and hope lie in an escape from Fate or Fortune (*anankē; tychē*) and from the astrological powers that enslave people and block their entrance to the heavenly sphere. The Hellenistic age has often been called an age of anxiety (Dodds[69]) or an age of failure of nerve (Murray[70]). Notwithstanding the Pax Romana, its civil order of law, and the fair imperial administration of the provinces, factors like the cosmopolitan atmosphere, the breakdown of natural boundaries and the waning of ethnic religions, the syncretism of East and West, and the social insecurity and anomie of the lower classes all combined to create a Gnostic climate of thought that emptied life of meaning. A cosmological dualism matches an anthropology that in Platonic fashion splits body and soul, matter and spirit, and considers the material body irrelevant, if not harmful, to people's communion with the divine and to their heavenly destiny.[71] A mentality prevails in which people feel alienated from their past and anxious about their future.

Within this context, the Corinthians have received the gospel with its message of the resurrection (1 Cor. 15:1, 2; "*episteusate*," v. 11). A breakdown of communications now ensues because of the different ideological backgrounds of the parties involved. The Corinthians deem salvation a present reality (cf. 1 Cor. 1:18: "*tois de sōzomenois ēmin*"; cf. 15:2); they know themselves to participate in Christ, who has conquered the powers that rule this world and has opened a way to the heavenly world of the Spirit. They have heard Paul's gospel of freedom from the world and its powers, which Christ has accomplished, and know themselves sacramentally united with him. They accept Paul's teaching that "all things are yours . . . the world or life or death or the present or the future . . . and you are Christ's; and Christ is God's" (1 Cor. 3:21–23; 6:11). This new knowledge (8:1) enables them to consider "all things lawful" (6:12; 10:23), that is, all things are indifferent to their new spiritual status. They believe that their measure of freedom in the gospel is dependent on their spiritual knowledge of the gospel (*gnōsis*). Moreover, their worship is one great joyful celebration of their spiritual gifts and a token of their spiritual transformation (chapter 14). Salvation means salvation from the body and from entanglement in a meaningless world. The resurrection of Christ is the apex of their religiosity. For here death has been overcome, and the Spirit has poured out on them the gift of eternal life. Resurrection power is existentially appropriated, and participation with Christ is realized through the sacraments of baptism and the Eucharist. The resurrection confirms the break between the ages, as Paul had said, and consequently the break with the material world, which after all is under the dominion of death and the hostile powers that Christ has overcome. When Paul spoke about "the god of this world" (2 Cor. 4:4), he confirmed a radical dualism between the world of the flesh and the world of the Spirit. And if "flesh and blood cannot inherit the kingdom of God, nor the perishable inherit the imperishable" (1 Cor. 15:50), then resurrection power sheds all that is material and knows the death and resurrection of Christ as the crucial moment of leaving "the earthly tent" (2 Cor. 5:1) for the "building from God, a house not made with hands, eternal in the heavens" (5:1). The resurrection of Christ means his spiritual ascent, and those in Christ are the spiritual elite; they are the "chosen ones" (1:2, 9, 26–29) who have already been united with the heavenly Lord and now wait for physical death as the moment of spiritual completion and the shedding of the body, because those who belong to Christ are already "one Spirit with him" (6:17). Within this setting of pneumatic freedom and ontological participation in Christ, the Corinthians bear witness to the gospel by demonstrating their freedom and by an ethic that proclaims in word and deed that they have become indifferent to the world and that history and human affairs, that is, bodily structures, cannot compromise and contaminate their mystic bond with Christ. In terms of their theology, then, a resurrection of the dead (i.e., a resurrection of dead bodies) is both disgusting (because the body is inimical to salvation) and unnecessary (because our spiritual union with Christ is the redemption of our true self).

## Paul's Argument

Paul's apocalyptic argument collides with the Hellenistic, enthusiastic world view of the Corinthians. He argues as follows (1 Cor. 15:12–22): (1) The resurrection of Christ from the dead (*ek nekrōn*)—that is, from Sheol and the realm of dead bodies—necessarily implies a final resurrection of the dead (*anastasis nekrōn*; v. 12). (2) If there is no final resurrection of the dead, then there is no resurrection of

Christ (v. 13). (3) If there is no resurrection of Christ, then there is no gospel or faith (v. 14). In verses 15, 16, and 17 the argument repeats itself: (1) If the dead are not raised, then God has not raised Christ (vv. 15, 16). (2) If Christ is not raised, then there is no gospel and no hope (vv. 17–19). Verse 20 concludes the argument of verses 12–19: "But in fact Christ has been raised from the dead, the first fruits of those who have fallen asleep."[72] The resurrection of Christ has no isolated or "completed" meaning. Although the death of Christ is a "once and for all event," the resurrection of Christ is not "completed" in its full meaning and consequence until the future resurrection of the dead. Therefore, the resurrection of Christ cannot be asserted apart from the future apocalyptic resurrection, because it derives its meaning from its future referent (cf. Rom. 1:4). Verses 20–28 undergird this assertion more specifically; verse 20 and verses 23–28 protect the Adam typology of verses 21 and 22 against an interpretation in terms of realized eschatology. The resurrection of Christ is here interpreted as the "first fruits of those who have fallen asleep" (v. 20), that is, as the first in a series to come (cf. "the first-born among many brethren," Rom. 8:29; "the first-born from the dead," Col. 1:18). It is not an event in the midst of history but rather the event that inaugurates the end of history. And because it is a historical and "material" event for which witnesses are listed (1 Cor. 15:1–11), the nature and mode of the final resurrection in the age to come require further elaboration. Therefore, Paul discusses the question "How are the dead raised? With what kind of body do they come?" (v. 35).[73] Because the end of history is not simply history's annihilation but its transformation, there is a body that will be raised and not just a disembodied Spirit, just as there will be a radical change (v. 51: *allagēsometha*) for the living and not a negation of the body. The relation between this age and the age of glory causes difficulties for Paul as for any apocalyptic writer, because the discontinuity of "the spiritual body" with the earthly body of "flesh and blood" (v. 50) readily suggests a radical dualism between historical and posthistorical existence. However, Paul's insistence on "change" (v. 51), on the continuity of personal identity (1 Thess. 4:15), and on the somatic character of the resurrection indicates a temperate dualism and a preservation of the historical self in the midst of the end-time transformation. Paul shares a lack of clarity on this point with apocalyptic thought in general, for which the "glory" of the new age indicates the radically new character of eternal life (cf. Apocalypse of Baruch 49–51; Mark 12:25: "like angels in heaven").[74] However, Paul's occasionally severe discontinuous language about life in the age to come should not deceive us (cf. "food is meant for the stomach and the stomach for food—and God will destroy both one and the other"; 1 Cor. 6:13). Paul's ethical imperatives, for instance, presuppose the transformation, rather than the futile destiny, of the created order: "The body is not meant for immortality, but for the Lord, and the Lord for the body. And God raised the Lord and will also raise us up by his power" (1 Cor. 6:13–14). And because the risen Christ has "a body of glory" (Phil. 3:21), which is continuous with the identity of Jesus, Paul is able to witness to the transformation of reality in the age of glory, because that age will not negate the created order but rather bring it to its eschatological destiny.

## Critical Evaluation

The circular nature of Paul's argument in 1 Cor. 15:12–19 is obvious and demonstrates the logical interaction between the two foci of the resurrection of Christ and the final apocalyptic resurrection. The cogency of the argument rests on a premise that is seemingly not open to discussion. However, this premise is for the Corinthians undoubtedly the questionable postulate that determines everything else. In other words, Paul's circular argument lacks a sufficient warrant, because what needs to be argued is taken for granted. Thus, Paul treats the warrant as an axiomatic premise because the very question of the Corinthians is taken for granted by Paul, that is, the necessary connection between the resurrection of Christ (which they affirm) and the futurity and materiality of a general resurrection (which they deny).

"The apocalyptic connection," then, constitutes the basis of Paul's argument (15:20–28). The spiritualist interpretation of the resurrection by the Corinthians, which later became the battleground between the church and gnosticism and was so appealing to a Greek-Platonic climate of thought, is simply cast aside by Paul's apocalyptic world view. The Corinthians argue that because Christ's resurrection was a resurrection from death, it constituted his victory over death. Why, then, should the resurrection of Christ from death/from the dead[75] mean a resurrection (or a resuscitation) of dead bodies?[76] In many New Testament hymns the resurrection of Christ signifies Christ's victory over death and his status as world ruler, *kosmokrator*, that is, it means his exaltation and not specifically a "bodily" resurrection. Rather, the resurrection here celebrates simply the enthronement of Christ as "Lord," and there is no reference to Christ as the "first fruits" of the general resurrection of the dead.

Moreover, 1 Cor. 15:45 speaks about the risen Christ as "a life-giving Spirit" without mentioning his "spiritual body," and Paul refers to the "spiritual body" only in 1 Cor. 15:44 (cf. vv. 35–49; Phil. 3:21). The "image" concept (*eikōn*; 1 Cor. 15:49) does not necessarily suggest materiality, as its adoption by later Gnostics indicates. And Paul's references to the church as "Christ" (1 Cor. 12:12) and as "the body of Christ" might have suggested to the Corinthians that the body of the risen Lord was the church, that is, the body of believers rather than a heavenly spiritual body.

It is curious indeed that Paul's specific "resurrection body" argument (1 Cor. 15:35–49) is not set forth more clearly. The Corinthians could have accepted (in spiritualistic terms) the assertions of verses 35–41; the analogies of seed and grain and of the different kinds of bodies could easily be spiritualized. The stumbling block occurs when analogy shifts to ontology in verses 42–49: "It is sown a physical body, it is raised a spiritual body" (v. 44).

In other words, Paul himself is not too outspoken about a "spiritual body." He presupposes it more than he argues it (except for 1 Cor.

15:44). Thus, its rare usage by Paul leads to the possible misunderstanding that redemption is *from* the body (but cf. Rom. 8:23) and that there is no need for a heavenly body (2 Cor. 5:6–9; Phil. 1:21–23). The Corinthians may have had not only a more consistent logic than Paul but also a foothold in Christian tradition when they interpreted Christ's resurrection as his (bodiless?) exaltation to heaven.

The difficulty of belief in the resurrection of the body is vividly expressed in later Valentinian-Gnostic circles, where the belief in bodily resurrection is called "the faith of fools" (i.e., the psychics).[77] If sacramental logic dictates that cocrucifixion with Christ means death to the body of sin and death (Rom. 6:6; 7:24), then coresurrection with Christ means necessarily participation in the life of the spiritual Christ (see Chapter 10 in my *Paul the Apostle*). Why, then, does "being in Christ" have to be contradicted by a renewal of corporeality, which in fact is a basic obstacle to union with God? Are not both cocrucifixion and coresurrection profound "images," not to be taken literally? Did not Paul himself argue in Romans 6 that our crucifixion with Christ means our death with him and our resurrection with Christ our newness of life and our future "life" with him (Rom. 6:8: *suzēsomen*)? And if the resurrection of Christ is his exaltation to God's right hand and a shedding of his material body on the cross, what is so religiously important about a resurrection of dead bodies? Such an expectation destroys the enjoyment and meaning of the full blessing of redemption. The "exaltation" theology of the Corinthians has indeed a consistent logic. Paul counters it, for example, in 1 Cor. 15:22. We expect "For as by a man came death, by a man also came *life*," but instead we read in the last clause, "By a man has come also *the resurrection of the dead*" (cf. Rom. 5:18–19, where no resurrection of the dead is mentioned).

## Paul's Dogmatic Imposition

At first glance Paul does not seem to "understand" the Corinthian position. This is due not to poor information[78] but obviously to a clash in ideologies. Nevertheless, Paul understands very well the religious-ethical consequences of the Corinthian position. He observes that party strife, lack of moral sensitivity, contempt for one's neighbor, and religious pride are not consistent with the gospel and the love of Christ. But why can't he understand that a Hellenistic-Gentile church must base its Christian gospel and ethic on a world view that is conso-nant with its own culture? In other words, are Christian theology and ethics necessarily bound to a world view that is alien to its recipients, and is the gospel itself bound to the contingency and cultural relativity of a particular world view? Why, then, does Paul impose an apocalyptic world view on Gentiles and so run the risk of confusing the heart of the gospel with a system of thought that is, after all, culturally deter-mined and cannot claim any "abiding" divine truth? How can Paul, in 1 Corinthians 15, ascribe religious and moral failure to the rejection of the apocalyptic world view? Is he so ideologically caught in his own world view that he fails to acknowledge that the gospel must tolerate a variety of world views? Is he ignorant about the Corinthian world view, or does he know it but refuse a hermeneutic of the gospel in its terms? Thus, he can even indict the Corinthian position as Epicureanism, that is, as an outright denial of eternal life, when he writes, "If the dead are not raised, 'Let us eat and drink, for tomorrow we die'" (1 Cor. 15:32). Likewise, he is puzzled by the Corinthian practice of baptism on behalf of dead relatives: "If the dead are not raised at all, why are people bap-tized on their behalf" (1 Cor. 15:29).

It is curious that Paul, so conscious of his universal call to be "the apostle to the Gentiles" (Rom. 11:13), insists on a particularist Jewish apocalyptic ideology to communicate the truth of the gospel in 1 Corinthians 15. How is it possible that he who stakes his apostolic career on the claim that the Gentile does not need to become a Jew (through circumcision and Torah) before becoming a Christian never-theless seems to insist that the Gentile must adopt a Jewish ideology or mentality in order to become a Christian? Does he not say,

*For though I am free from all men, I have made myself a*
*slave to all, that I might win the more. . . . To those outside*
*the law, I became as one outside the law . . . that I might*
*win those outside the law. . . . I have become all things to*
*all men, that I might by all means save some. I do it all*
*for the sake of the gospel, that I may share in its blessings*
*[1 Cor. 9:19–23].*

First Corinthians 15 provides us with an impressive example that
the coherent center of the gospel is, for Paul, not simply an experiential
reality of the heart or a Word beyond words that permits translation
into a multitude of world views. Harry Emerson Fosdick's dictum about
the gospel as an "abiding experience amidst changing world views," or
Bultmann's demythologizing program for the sake of the kerygmatic
address of the gospel, is in this manner not true to Paul's conception
of the gospel. However applicable the gospel must be to a Gentile in
his contingent situation, it does not tolerate a world view that cannot
express those elements inherent in the apocalyptic world view and that
to Paul seem inherent in the truth of the gospel (cf., e.g., the charge
of de Lagarde against Paul's introduction of rabbinic thought forms
into the simple gospel of Jesus[79]). Paul's gospel does seem welded to
the apocalyptic world view. And far from considering the apocalyptic
world view a husk or discardable frame, Paul insists that it belongs to
the inalienable coherent core of the gospel. The charge that Paul uni-
versalizes and absolutizes a cultural-temporal world view and makes it
normative for the truth of the gospel must be taken seriously, because
Paul connects the coherent center of the gospel with the particularity
of an apocalyptic idiom. It seems that Paul sacrifices dialogical contingency to dogmatic necessity by imposing a particular world view
on Hellenistic believers. And if Paul imposes a dogmatic interpretive
scheme on the "core" of the gospel, he seems to require not only faith
as *fiducia* but also faith as *assensus*, that is, as "assent" to a specific
world view. This seems to restrict severely the interaction between the

contingency and the coherent core of the gospel, that is, its character as language-event for a particular situation.

Indeed, according to Paul, the gospel is integrally connected with his apocalyptic world view: he cannot conceive of the resurrection of Christ—which the Corinthians affirm (1 Cor. 15:1, 2, 11)—apart from the apocalyptic general resurrection of the dead. Both stand or fall together. And it is not just a question of "communications"; it is not a linguistic problem that can be solved if only Paul can adjust his language and find a common ground. There are profound substantive issues involved in the language that concern the truth of the gospel. It seems that for Paul the apocalyptic world view is so interwoven with the truth of the gospel that if they are separated the gospel will be torn apart. If this is true, we have reached an important hermeneutical insight. Whenever apocalyptic categories are dismissed as husk or cultural accident or literal obsolescence, resurrection-language is transmuted into something else, for example, into the immortality of the soul, or our heavenly ascent, or into an existential possibility and especially into a denial of the created order. Thus, the rejection of apocalyptic categories as inconsistent with modernity and a scientific world view bears directly on the truth of the gospel! For Paul, the issue of "apocalyptic categories" is not a provincial idiosyncrasy but is interwoven with profound christological, anthropological, and ethical issues. Paul's problem with the Corinthians is at bottom their denial that spirituality is commensurate with materiality and historical existence. And this problem can only be solved, according to Paul, when the truth of the gospel (i.e., its coherent apocalyptic theme) is understood and appropriated.

As we will see, the interrelation of Spirit and body forms the basic theme of 1 Corinthians. The Spirit is for Paul determined by the apocalyptic future and does not signify the perfected state of present spirituality. It is the power that transforms the created order and directs it toward its consummation. When the Spirit is divorced from apocalyptic categories, it distorts the meaning of the gospel by unduly spiritualizing it. The Spirit, therefore, is connected with life in the body, with life for other bodies, and with eternal life as qualified by a body. And the totality of life in the body and for other bodies manifests itself concretely in the one "body of Christ," which constitutes the church. For that one ontological body of Christ does not mean an undifferentiated oneness of all who share the Spirit but rather the psycho-physical and cultural variety and mutual interdependence of its members, so that each member occupies a different function in the body (see Chapter 14 in my *Paul the Apostle*). Oneness "in Christ" does not neutralize the historical specificity of human "bodies" (notwithstanding Gal. 3:28). It is the historical particularity of each member in "the body of Christ" that makes love (*agape*) and upbuilding (*oikodome*) possible and necessary. Thus, the one body of Christ is not a pneumatic, ahistorical elite, but a communion of "diverse bodies" whose particularity must be respected (1 Cor. 12:14). Because the relation of spirituality to materiality in a historical context is the Corinthian problem, its solution is conceivable to Paul only in the apocalyptic structure of the gospel, for in this framework alone can the resurrection of Christ be correctly perceived in terms of its consequences for life in the body. This raises the hermeneutical question whether only an apocalyptic interpretation of the gospel can achieve Paul's program of correlating Spirit and body in the gospel.[80] If, however, "the resurrection of Christ" is the historically unique apostolic bedrock of the gospel, and if it is inseparably connected with the apocalyptic future—if, in other words, the resurrection within its apocalyptic coordinates is an event to which the Corinthians and all other Christians have access only in its apostolic and Pauline interpretation (1 Cor. 15:2)—then its translation into another world view (e.g., "Christ is alive again" or "Christ has conquered death") is insufficient. Indeed, the history of dogma shows that the loss of an apocalyptic interpretation of the resurrection of Christ (e.g., in categories of immortality or enthusiasm in the Spirit) leads to a perversion of the gospel because it ignores the temporal and cosmic coordinates of the resurrection of Christ. Paul, then, does not so much "misunderstand" the Corinthians but rather understands precisely the reason for their perversion of the gospel, that is, their rejection of its apocalyptic coordinates.

## 1 Corinthians 15 and the Theme of the Letter

Both 1 Corinthians as a whole and chapter 15 in particular raise fundamental questions about the nature of Paul's way of doing theology. In chapter 15 Paul seems to impose an apocalyptic world view on the nonapocalyptic world view of his audience and so to sacrifice dialogical contingency to a dogmatic conception of the coherent core of the gospel. Moreover, the letter as a whole reads like a series of contingent theological statements that do not seem to cohere into what we have claimed to be the coherent apocalyptic theme of Paul's gospel. When Karl Barth locates the coherent theme of 1 Corinthians in its climactic chapter 15, he makes an important contribution to the relation between contingency and coherent theme in the letter.[81] However, "the canon in the canon" of 1 Corinthians is not as easily established as Barth thinks.

Paul certainly does argue in such a contingent manner that the Corinthians may well have misinterpreted the coherent core of the gospel. The tradition that Paul inherited from Antioch centered on the death and resurrection of Christ (1 Cor. 15:3–5; cf. also 1:13, 18; 2:2; 6:14; 8:11). However, although 1 Cor. 15:3–5 explicitly cites the tradition of both the death and resurrection of Christ, Paul focuses solely on the resurrection clause in his interpretation of the gospel in chapter 15 ("he was raised on the third day," v. 4), and omits any explication of the death of Christ.

In 1 Corinthians 1 and 2, to the contrary, the gospel is interpreted solely in terms of the death (cross) of Christ, and there is no reference to the resurrection of Christ.[82] It seems that the diverse polemical situations of the letter compel Paul to such a diversity and contingency of argumentation that the death and resurrection of Christ are torn apart and the "whole" gospel of Paul, that is, its coherent core (cf. *to euangelion*, 15:1[83]) is thwarted. The contrast with Romans 6 is striking because here the integral unity of dying and rising with Christ is impressively explicated.

Barth's claim about 1 Corinthians 15 as the coherent core and key to the whole letter presupposes that at chapter 15 the readers still have chapters 1 and 2 clearly in mind and are able to integrate the different foci of these chapters. Paul's strategy comes as a surprise, because the death of Christ would have helped Paul to clarify the nature of the resurrection in chapter 15, as much as the resurrection of Christ would have helped him in his argument in chapters 1 and 2.

Paul's firm resolution "For I decided to know nothing among you except Jesus Christ and him crucified" (1 Cor. 2:2), which constitutes the heart of his gospel, is virtually ignored in chapter 15. Because the polemical edge of chapter 15 is directed against the enthusiastic life-style of the Corinthians, the message of cross and resurrection would have clarified the nature of the resurrection in chapter 15. For if the resurrection is primarily the victory over sin (Rom. 6:10) and a new service in the body (Rom. 6:12), the correlation of Spirit and life in the body, which the pneumatic Corinthians reject, is based on our participation in the death and resurrection of Christ (Rom. 6:1–10). In other words, if the resurrection of Christ is primarily a victory over sin and in that sense a victory over death, why doesn't 1 Corinthians 15 integrate sin and death and relate them to the cross and resurrection in such a way that the victory over death is more than a promise of a future resurrection-body, more than physical "survival" in the afterlife? Do we not have to say in terms of the argument of Romans 6 that victory over death is primarily a victory over sin (Rom. 6:10) because sin is "the sting of death" (1 Cor. 15:56)? And does not the cross of Christ signify precisely this victory over sin? The consequence of this victory is a new life of service to God in the body as "men who have been brought from death to life" (Rom. 6:13), a "newness of life" (Rom. 6:4) of those who after the destruction of the body of sin (Rom. 6:6) can now present their "bodies as a living sacrifice, holy and acceptable to God" (Rom. 12:1). The Corinthian divorce of Spirit and body could have been met by grounding the Christian ethic (in terms of a correlation of Spirit and body) in the death and resurrection of Christ. As it is now presented in 1 Corinthians 15, this ethic rests on the resurrection argument alone: the resurrection of Christ promises a future resurrection-body, so that the body is ethically significant—something the Corinthians deny.

Again, in 1 Corinthians 1 and 2, the resurrection of Christ could have assisted Paul in clarifying the cross as "God's power" (1 Cor. 1:24) and his own preaching as "the power of God and the demonstration of the Spirit" (2:1–5). In short, why is the resurrection as part of "the things of first importance" (*en prōtois*, 15:3) not the theme or a theme of chapters 1 and 2 as well, and why are these "things of first importance"—which include the death of Christ—interpreted in chapter 15 solely in terms of the resurrection and not in terms of Christ's death?

The interaction between coherent core and contingency is a definite problem in 1 Corinthians. Romans and 1 Corinthians seem very different in this respect. In Romans the coherent theme is quite clear, but its contingency is unclear; in 1 Corinthians the coherent theme is unclear, but its contingency is obvious. First Corinthians 15 presents a coherent apocalyptic core, but it seems as if Paul imposes a dogmatic structure on the Corinthians which disregards their contingent situation, that is, their nonapocalyptic world view. Again, a comparison of chapters 1 and 2 with chapter 15 shows a contingent argumentation throughout the letter which seems to disregard the "whole" of Paul's gospel, that is, the death (chapters 1 and 2) *and* resurrection of Christ (chapter 15).

We must remember, however, that the letter situation, with its contingent, exhortative, and polemical arguments, is quite different from Paul's first proclamation of the gospel to the Corinthians. Thus the letter situation represents a second-level dialogue that permits greater contingent emphases than were possible in Paul's first-level foundational proclamation: "I decided to know nothing among you except Jesus Christ and him crucified" (1 Cor. 2:2).

## Spirit and Body

In the light of Paul's contingent argument in 1 Corinthians, we can understand the partition theories to which the letter has been frequently subjected. Walter Schmithals,[84] for instance, assigns chapter 15 to an earlier letter (letter B), and thus isolates chapter 15 from the literary context of the whole letter, in order to explain the different emphases of chapter 1 (letter D: 1:1—4:21) and chapter 15 (letter B).[85]

Although such theories are worthy to be pursued, one wonders whether they are not an attempt to bypass the remarkable interaction in Paul between the coherent theme of the gospel and his contingent argumentation, for the letter reveals that its coherent theme revolves around the correlation of Spirit and body. The Corinthians adhere to the proposition that the material (the body) is inimical to the spiritual (the Spirit). They split apart what Paul conjoins. And so Paul consistently maintains the integration of body and Spirit throughout the letter (1 Cor. 3:16–17; 6:13–20; 9:24–27). Thus, the integration of Spirit and body in an apocalyptic perspective provides the contingent interpretation of the gospel in the Corinthian situation.

I conclude, then, that chapter 15, with its apocalyptic focus on the resurrection and its emphasis on the ultimate significance of the resurrection-body, is indeed the climax of that interpretation of the gospel that the Corinthians had to hear according to Paul. The coherent center of the gospel is in 1 Corinthians unfolded as the correlation of Spirit and body, in the light of the apocalyptic resurrection-body. To Paul, the rejection of this theme by the Corinthians means that they have rejected the gospel. Therefore, Barth is indeed correct when he claims 1 Corinthians 15 as the key to Paul's letter.[86] However, its relation to chapters 1 and 2 is more tenuous than he thinks. This applies as well to Käsemann's statement about 1 Corinthians 15: "The Risen Exalted One remains the Crucified One."[87] The resurrection of the crucified Christ may well have been the subject of Paul's foundational preaching and the underlying presupposition of the letter, but the literary structure of the letter itself does not show it.

## Conclusion: Chronology and Theology

It cannot be too strongly emphasized that Paul's thought is motivated by the future consummation as God's goal with history and creation. All the ingredients of Paul's thought find their proper location only within this futurist flow. Our modern distaste for Paul's apocalyptic conceptuality thus distorts our focus. What to us is husk and peripheral is primary to Paul, and what to us is kernel and core is differently focused in Paul. Although Christocentrism seems a true description of Paul's thought, it leads to distortions if we ignore Paul's theocentric-apocalyptic posture. Wrede comments:

> *The whole Pauline conception of salvation is characterized by suspense; a suspense which strains forward towards the final release, the actual death. The earthly life is not the setting in which salvation becomes complete. In this connection we should keep before our minds with especial clearness a fact which, indeed, when we are dealing with Paul, ought never to be forgotten. He believed with all his might in the speedy coming of Christ and the approaching end of the world. In consequence, the redemptive act of Christ, which lay in the past and the dawn of the future glory lay, in his view, close together. . . . It has been popularly held that Paul departed from the view of salvation of the early Church by shifting the stress from the future to the past, looking upon the blessedness of the Christian as already attained, and emphasizing faith instead of hope. It is easy to see that this is assuredly but a half truth. All references to the redemption as a completed transaction swing around at once into utterances about the future. . . . There are deep-reaching differences between*

*the Pauline doctrine of redemption and the thoughts of modern belief.*[88]

First Corinthians 15 shows clearly the necessary relation between the resurrection of Christ and the final resurrection of the dead. The chronological proximity of this relation contains a theological necessity. On the one hand, the resurrection of Christ is a sign of the impending kingdom (1 Cor. 15:24); on the other hand, the general resurrection of the dead is the completion of the resurrection of Christ. For Paul, then, the Christ-event is at once crucial and provisional. The analogy of D-Day and V-Day illustrates this. A D-Day without an impending V-Day loses its character of D-Day. Likewise, a D-Day that is celebrated as if it were V-Day loses sight of the reality of things because it ignores God's plan of cosmic redemption and is caught in an overheated spiritualistic illusion, "as if the day of the Lord *has* come" (2 Thess. 2:2). D-Day is provisional, but it is also crucial. The Corinthians, however, with their spiritual pride, celebrate D-Day as if it were V-Day. Thus they claim for the present what God has ordained for the future and disdain historical existence and its concrete demands with their individualist mysticism.[89]

The interpreters of consistent eschatology (Albert Schweitzer, Martin Werner, Fritz Buri[90]) deserve credit for pointing to this futurist-eschatological element in the New Testament as a whole. Their critics have correctly noted that if future eschatology were such a decisive matter, the delay of the Parousia would have destroyed Christian faith. Thus, Oscar Cullmann characterized Christ as "the center" (*die Mitte der Zeit*) of Christian faith and eschatology as a variable that was and is constantly open to shifting emphases.[91] Werner, to the contrary, argues that de-eschatologizing is the key to the development of Christian dogma.[92] It is unfortunate that the problem of the future theocentric thrust of Paul became so heavily centered on the question of chronology, that is, on the delay of the Parousia. That debate concludes prematurely that, inasmuch as the Parousia has not taken place, the center of Christian faith either lies in Christology or calls for an existentialist resolution of the early Christian hope. In fact, Paul can adjust himself remarkably well to the delay of the Parousia. If there is any "development" in his thinking, it certainly concerns the issue of its arrival. Whereas he expects to be alive at the Parousia in 1 Thess. 4:15 and 1 Cor. 15:50–52, he seems to contemplate his death before its occurrence in Phil. 1:20 and possibly in 2 Cor. 5:1–11 (cf. 2 Cor. 1:9). Even so, he can write in what was one of his last letters, "Salvation is nearer to us now than when we first believed" (Rom. 13:11; cf. Phil. 4:4). In other words, he persists in imminent expectation, notwithstanding his awareness of the delay of the Parousia. His response to the excited Thessalonians shows a restraint against chronological expectations and calculations: "But as to the times and the seasons, brethren, you have no need to have anything written to you. For you yourselves know well that the day of the Lord will come like a thief in the night" (1 Thess. 5:1, 2). Although the usual indictment against apocalyptic with its calculations and timetables seems a gross exaggeration,[93] Paul's deviation from this apocalyptic practice is obvious. A similar observation can be drawn from Paul's missionary method, because it reveals no contradiction between apocalyptic fervor and missionary strategy. Paul is simply not an apocalyptic fanatic who runs breathlessly through the Roman Empire because the end of the world is imminent. He spends, for instance, one and a half years at Corinth and three years at Ephesus and contemplates a mission to Spain. Thus, eschatology and missions do not contradict each other, as if the one paralyzes the strength of the other. The mission charge in Acts 1:6–8 is much more concerned with the alternative—eschatology *or* missions—than anything in Paul. Paul can contemplate a universal mission and yet live in terms of apocalyptic imminence. It seems, therefore, that the scholarly debate on the delay of the Parousia focuses exclusively on calculating chronological time, that is, on the chronological dating that separates the Christ-event and the end time, whereas for Paul the issue is primarily not one of chronological reckoning but one of theological necessity. Chronological proximity is important as the concomitant of theological necessity, because there is a necessary relation between the "already" and the "not yet" in the gospel. It is interesting that Bultmann interprets the chronological tension in existentialist terms and thus in terms of theological necessity. However, he confuses chronological reckoning with chronological expectation, and his anthropological hermeneutic loses sight of the cosmic dimensions of the Christian hope. Thus, he ignores the "not yet" of the transformation of the creation and the "not yet" of God's final verdict on our responsibility in the last judgment. According to Paul, Christians can never surrender the universal-cosmic future horizon of the Christ-event, and the imminence of God's kingdom, if they consider the resurrection of Christ to be of fundamental importance to their faith. Indeed, the resurrection prompts Christians to an apocalyptic self-understanding in the world. For in their own bodies Christians live existentially the tension of their present incompleted existence in solidarity with an unredeemed creation, and they must therefore yearn for the consummation of the resurrection, which is nothing but God's triumph over the power of death that poisons his creation. It may be argued that the phenomenon of hope in human life points to the need for a completion that will enable us to understand fully what we now only understand fragmentarily (1 Cor. 13:12; cf. Pannenberg). This completion will resolve the tension of our present life in the body, because our lives can be complete only when they embrace our contradictions as well as those of the created order. Only then will "the last enemy," death, be swallowed up (2 Cor. 5:4) by life and by the triumph of God (see Chapter 16 in my *Paul the Apostle*). In this light the often maligned theology of 2 Peter is in some ways on the right track, because for Peter the chronological delay of the Parousia does not mean its theological demise (2 Pet. 3:8–10).

Both the great importance and the provisionality of the Christ-event must be maintained, just as D-Day cannot be without V-Day. The Christ-event itself is misappropriated if it is not seen as the proleptic anticipation of the age to come. It is a mistake to introduce here a philosophical hermeneutic, as if Paul understands the relation between the Christ-event and the kingdom of God in terms of antinomy, paradox, or in dialectical terms, that is, within the Greek cyclical understanding of time.[94] The tension between the resurrection of Christ and the general resurrection cannot be defined without its chronological and cosmic-universal dimension. Otherwise, the apocalyptic tension becomes subject to docetic distortion. For Paul, the temporal element is necessary for the sake of the cosmic hope of the creation. Just as the "not yet" of the temporal dimension safeguards the cosmic nature of the future eschatological event, the "already" of the Christ-event announces its imminence. A philosophical interpretation of the relation between the Christ-event and the final glory of God in terms of dialectics and paradox constitutes a denial of the character of the Parousia as future event in Paul, because it transforms the expectation of an ontic event into a noetic perception and interprets it as a perennial religious tension.

The question raised by 1 Corinthians 15 is why Paul insists on an apocalyptic world view as an inherent part of the gospel. If the basic problem in 1 Corinthians is the nature of Christian life as life in the body by the Spirit, a theology of the cross, as developed in chapters 1 and 2, might have provided a sufficient solution to the Corinthian problem of a prematurely realized eschatology in the Spirit. In fact, the Gospel of John shows us the possibility of such a position. Here the cross itself becomes the moment of glorification, whereas "cross-bearing" characterizes Christian life and heavenly immortality its victory (John 15:18–25; 16:2–4, 33; 17:14–19). Why then does Paul's "eschatological reservation" need an apocalyptic world view? Can it not be sustained by Christian life "under the cross"? A simple affirmation of that question is inadequate. A theology of the cross that is unrelated to the resurrection as "first fruits" of the kingdom of God and the future resurrection of the dead is in danger of neglecting the created order and the hope for God's final cosmic victory over his rebellious creation, which he promised in the resurrection of Christ. In that case, the theology of the cross is easily transformed into a passion mysticism and the resurrection into the noetic meaning of the victory of the cross (cf. Bultmann). The Gospel of John shows the limitation of such a theology of the cross, because—notwithstanding Christian life under the cross—the cross becomes the secret hour of glory, the "gateway" to heaven, and it ceases to have cosmic-eschatological meaning for a fallen world. Thus, in Paul the cross is embedded in the apocalyptic framework of the resurrection of Christ, so that the proleptic victory of the cross and resurrection moves toward the future public victory of God in the final resurrection. Christian life in the body by the Spirit is indeed life under the cross. Therefore, we "proclaim the death of the Lord" in the Eucharist (1 Cor. 11:26). But life under the cross is not celebrated as if suffering has become acceptable or "good" in the gospel. Life under the cross awaits God's victory, and so Paul adds, we "proclaim the Lord's death until he comes" (1 Cor. 11:26). The "eschatological reservation" expects the future resurrection of the dead, so that the present paradox of victory *amid* death (2 Cor. 4:11) can be sustained by the hope in the transformation of all creation, that is, in the victory *over* death. Only then the song of triumph will be heard: "Death is swallowed up in victory" (1 Cor. 15:54). The "redemption of the body" (Rom. 8:23) is not a "redemption from the body" but a redemption of the total "body" of creation (Rom. 8:21). And so Paul concludes, "Therefore, my beloved brethren, be steadfast, immovable, always abounding in the work of the Lord, knowing that in the Lord your labor is not in vain" (1 Cor. 15:58).

The apocalyptic world view is the fundamental carrier of Paul's thought. Without it his basic christological focus becomes distorted. Without it the design of Paul's theology shifts from Christ as "first fruits" to Christ as the total "fulness of God" (Col. 1:19), that is, Christ as that total and completed revelation of God which exhausts all God's glory and triumph. For Paul, the "material content" (*Sachgehalt*) of the gospel is inseparable from the necessary "linguistic medium" (*Sprachgestalt*) of apocalyptic thought; in fact, the coherent theme of the gospel is unthinkable apart from apocalyptic. In that sense, apocalyptic thought patterns are not to be demythologized or regarded as incidental linguistic "husk" that can be transposed into a nonapocalyptic metaphysic. The post-Pauline history of the church shows abundantly that the gospel itself was jeopardized when nonapocalyptic thought forms became its hermeneutical carrier.

It is interesting that Christian hermeneutics has regularly adopted the dualistic component of apocalyptic—in whatever spiritualistic or existentialist terms—whereas it has neglected and/or obscured its other two components, imminence and cosmic-universalism. And so it has failed to understand Paul properly, because the dimensions of imminence and cosmic expectation are central to Paul, whereas that of apocalyptic dualism is tempered by the salvation-historical understanding of Israel's place in God's saving design for his creation.

## Notes

1  William Morgan, *The Religion and Theology of Paul*, p. 6.
2  Philipp Vielhauer, "Introduction [to Apocalypses and Related Subjects]," in *New Testament Apocrypha*.
3  Klaus Koch, *The Rediscovery of Apocalyptic*, pp. 18–35.
4  Vielhauer, "Introduction."
5  Koch, *Rediscovery of Apocalyptic*, pp. 28–32.
6  Julius Wellhausen, "Zur apokalyptischen Literatur," in *Skizzen und Vorarbeiten*.
7  Dietrich Rössler, *Gesetz und Geschichte*; Frank Moore Cross, *The Ancient Library of Qumran and Modern Biblical Studies*, p. 54, n. 33.
8  George Foot Moore, *Judaism in the First Centuries of the Christian Era*.
9  Wilhelm Bousset, *Die Religion des Judentums im späthellenistischen Zeitalter*.
10  Rössler, *Gesetz und Geschichte*.

11 Flavius Josephus *The Jewish War* 2. 259ff.; idem, *The Antiquities of the Jews* 18–20.

12 Louis Ginsburg, "Some Observations on the Attitude of the Synagogue towards the Apocalyptic-Eschatological Writings," p. 134.

13 Ibid.

14 Cf., e.g., William David Davies, "The Jewish Background of the Teaching of Jesus," in *Christian Origins and Judaism*; Ed Parish Sanders, *Paul and Palestinian Judaism*.

15 E.g., Ginsburg, "Some Observations on the Attitude of the Synagogue," p. 134.

16 Cf. Vielhauer, "Introduction."

17 Albert Schweitzer, *The Mysticism of Paul*; Martin Werner, *Die Entstehung des christlichen Dogmas*.

18 Wellhausen, "Zur apokalyptischen Literatur"; Bernhard Duhm, *Israels Propheten*, p. 460; cf. Koch, *Rediscovery of Apocalyptic*, pp. 36ff.

19 Rudolf Schnackenburg, *God's Rule and Kingdom*, p. 69.

20 David Friedrich Strauss, *The Life of Jesus, Critically Examined*.

21 Charles Harold Dodd, *New Testament Studies*, pp. 67–128.

22 Morgan, *Religion and Theology of Paul*, p. 5.

23 Rudolf Karl Bultmann, "New Testament and Mythology," in *Kerygma and Myth*, vol. 1, esp. pp. 12ff.

24 Rudolf Karl Bultmann, *Primitive Christianity in Its Contemporary Setting*, p. 186.

25 Ibid.

26 Ibid., p. 184.

27 Rudolf Karl Bultmann, *Theology of the New Testament*, 1:322.

28 Ibid., 2:175ff.

29 Cf. Paul Ricoeur's critique (in "Préface à Bultmann," in *Le Conflict des Interprétations*) of Bultmann's attempt to search behind the language for its real intent.

30 John Goodrich Gager, "Functional Diversity in Paul's Use of End-Time Language."

31 Karl Barth, *Der Römerbrief*, p. 298; E.T., p. 314.

32 Paul Althaus, *Die letzten Dinge*, p. 272.

33 Jürgen Moltmann, *Theology of Hope*; Wolfhart Pannenberg, *Jesus—God and Man*.

34  Ernst Käsemann, "On the Subject of Primitive Christian Apocalyptic"; idem, "The Beginnings of Christian Theology," in *New Testament Questions of Today*; Peter Stuhlmacher, *Gerechtigkeit Gottes bei Paulus*; idem, "Erwägungen zum Problem von Gegenwart und Zukunft in der paulinischen Theologie"; Ulrich Wilckens, "Die Bekehrung des Paulus als religionsgeschichtliches Problem"; Hans Joachim Schoeps, *Paul*; William David Davies, *Paul and Rabbinic Judaism*; Sanders, *Paul and Palestinian Judaism*; Paul David Hanson, *The Dawn of Apocalyptic*.

35  Käsemann, "Beginnings of Christian Theology," in *New Testament Questions of Today*, p. 102.

36  Koch, *Rediscovery of Apocalyptic*, p. 47.

37  Schweitzer, *Mysticism of Paul*; Bousset, *Die Religion des Judentums*. Bousset exempts Jesus from apocalyptic and is followed in this by many other New Testament scholars.

38  Leonhard Goppelt, "Apokalyptik und Typologie bei Paulus."

39  Willi Marxsen, *Introduction to the New Testament*, p. 273.

40  Hans Georg Conzelmann, "Zur Analyse der Bekenntnisformel I. Kor. 15,3–5"; cf. also Ernst Fuchs, "Über die Aufgabe einer christlichen Theologie."

41  Sanders, *Paul and Palestinian Judaism*, p. 543.

42  Jörg Baumgarten, *Paulus und die Apokalyptik*.

43  However, this concept is not documented in Jewish literature until A.D. 135.

44  Only Ephesians employs this terminology: Eph. 2:7 *aiōnes* (plural) *eperchomenoi*; Eph. 1:21: *ho aiōn mellōn*; Eph. 2:2; 3:9; 6:12; cf. also Matt. 13:32 vs. Mark 3:29.

45  Only Gal. 1:4 implies with "the present evil aeon" (cf. 2 Cor. 4:4: "the god of this age," trans. mine; cf. Rom. 12:2; 1 Cor. 1:20; 2:6, 8; 3:18), the *future* of the new age to come.

46  References to "the day [of the Lord; of Christ]" occur most often in traditional contexts: 1 Thess. 3:10; 5:2, 4; Rom. 2:5, 16; 13:12; 1 Cor. 1:8; 3:13; 5:5; 2 Cor. 1:14; Phil. 1:6, 10; 2:16.

47  Rudolf Karl Bultmann, *"Elpis."*

48  Bultmann, *Primitive Christianity*, p. 186.

49  Jürgen Becker, *Das Heil Gottes*, pp. 58ff.; Heinz Wolfgang Kuhn, *Enderwartung und gegenwärtiges Heil*, pp. 44–175.

50 Cf. esp: Stuhlmacher, "Erwägungen zum Problem von Gegenwart und Zukunft."

51 Cf. Ulrich Luz, "Der alte und der neue Bund bei Paulus und im Hebräerbrief."

52 Cf. Luke 24:39; Tertullian *De resurrectione carnis*; Luther's Commentary on 1 Corinthians 15; Georg Kretschmar, "Auferstehung des Fleisches," in *Leben Angesicht des Todes*.

53 E.g., Bultmann, *Primitive Christianity*, p. 186.

54 Bultmann, "New Testament and Mythology."

55 Ernst Käsemann, "On Paul's Anthropology," in *Perspectives on Paul*.

56 Bultmann, *Theology of the New Testament*, 1:viii and chaps. 4 and 5.

57 Ibid., pp. 270ff.

58 Cf. also the glorification on the Mount (Mark 9:1–8) and the stories of Jesus walking on the sea as composed of resurrection traditions. Cf. also Luke 5:1–11, originally the resurrection appearance to Peter?

59 George Bertram, "Die Himmelfahrt Jesu vom Kreuz aus und der Glaube an seine Auferstehung," in *Festgabe für Adolf Deissmann*, p. 202.

60 Walter Bauer, *Das Leben Jesu im Zeitalter der neutestamentlichen Apokryphen*, p. 253.

61 1Qh 12:11, 12; 13:19; 14:13; 16:9, 11, 12, etc.

62 Oscar Cullmann, *Christ and Time*, p. 145.

63 Archibald Macbride Hunter, *Interpreting Paul's Gospel*, p. 127.

64 For a different interpretation, cf. Andreas Lindemann, "Zurn Abfassungszweck des Zweiten Thessalonicherbriefes"; cf. also Gerhard Friedrich, "1 Thessalonicher 5,1–11," in *Auf das Wort kommt es an.*

65 Both Luke and Matthew adopt a similar "postponement" strategy; cf. Luke 18:1; 21:9; 19:11; 17:20; Matt. 25:1–13, 19; 24:48.

66 Elaine Hiesey Pagels, *The Gnostic Paul*; cf. also Malcolm Lee Peel, *The Epistle to Rheginos*.

67 Karl Barth, *The Resurrection of the Dead*, pp. 13–124.

68 Cf. Peter von der Osten-Sachen, "Gottes Treue bis zur Parusie."

69 Eric Robertson Dodds, *Pagan and Christian in an Age of Anxiety*.

70 George Murray, *Five Stages of Greek Religion*.

71   The aesthetic pleasure of the beauty of the body in classic Hellenism is turned into its opposite in Hellenistic religion.

72   Paul confuses here his own apocalyptic premise with that of the Corinthians; they did not deny the resurrection of Christ and would have agreed with Paul's claims in 1 Cor. 15:17–19.

73   Joachim Jeremias ("'Flesh and Blood Cannot Inherit the Kingdom of God,'" p. 158) argues that 1 Cor. 15:50 does not mean a spiritualization of the resurrection, that it speaks rather about the change of the living at the Parousia.

74   According to the Apocalypse of Baruch 49–51, the dead are raised in their earthly state in order to secure their identity (50:3). Only after the judgment are the righteous changed.

75   "Christ has been raised from the dead" (*ek nekrōn egēgertai*, 1 Cor. 15:12–30). Elsewhere, simply "he has been raised" in 1 Cor. 15:4 (creed!), 14, 16, 17; or "God raised Christ" (1 Cor. 15:15). Resurrection language is often synonymous with exaltation language, and the victory over death and the powers is associated with it: Phil. 2:7: "God has highly exalted him"; 2 Tim. 1:10: "who has abolished death and has brought life and immortality to light"; 1 Tim. 3:16: "vindicated in the Spirit, seen by angels, . . . taken up in glory"; 1 Pet. 3:18: "being put to death in the flesh but made alive in the Spirit"; 1 Pet. 3:22: resurrection means "has gone into heaven and is at the right hand of God, with angels, authorities, and powers subject to him"; Heb. 2:9: "Jesus . . . crowned with glory and honor because of the suffering of death, so that . . . he might taste death for every one"; Heb. 2:14: ". . . that through death he might destroy him who has the power of death, that is, the devil."

76   "Resurrection of dead [bodies]" (*anastasis nekrōn*, i.e., *sōmatōn*); cf. 1 Cor. 15:35–43; Dan. 12:2; Isa. 26:19: "their bodies shall rise"; cf. also Rom. 1:4: "*ex anastaseōs nekrōn.*"

77   Pagels, *The Gnostic Paul*, p. 84.

78   Cf. Walter Schmithals, *Die Gnosis in Korinth*.

79   Paul Anton de Lagarde, *Deutsche Schriften*.

80   For example, a correlation not in terms of the apocalyptic future but in terms of the cross of Christ as the basis for ethical life (i.e., the body as locus of the cross and cross-bearing [2 Cor. 4:10–11]).

81 Barth, *Resurrection of the Dead*, pp. 13–124.

82 Compare the following discussion of themes in 1 Corinthians with the themes of Jürgen Moltmann in the *Theology of Hope* and in *The Crucified God*. Precisely how are "the resurrection of the crucified Christ" and "the cross of the risen Christ" related? How is the suffering of God in the Son and with us related to the triumph of God in the resurrection of Christ and in the final kingdom? Why are the apocalyptic coordinates of the *Theology of Hope* so subordinated to the suffering love of God in *The Crucified God*? Does Moltmann disjoin here the themes of the cross and the resurrection, a disjunction not unlike Paul's when we compare 1 Corinthians 1 and 2 to 1 Corinthians 15?

83 Paul refers to "the gospel" as such in 1 Cor. 15:1, yet in 1 Cor. 2:2 that gospel seems to be "Jesus Christ and him crucified" as Paul's particular gospel to the Corinthians.

84 Walter Schmithals, "Die Korintherbriefe als Briefsammlung."

85 Schmithals (ibid.) divides as follows (I=1 Corinthians; II=2 Corinthians):
   Brief A: I 11:2–34
   Brief B: I 6:1–11 and II 6:14—7:1 and I 6:12–20 and
      9:24—10:22 and 15:1–58 and 16:13–24 *(Vorbrief)*
   Brief C: I 5:1–13 and 7:1—8:13 and 9:14–22 and
      10:23—11:1 and 12:1–31a and 14:1c–40 and
      12:31b—13:13 and 16:1–12 *(Antwortbrief)*
   Brief D: I 1:1—4:21 (cf. Dahl on the importance of 1 Cor.
      1–4 in: "Paul and the Church at Corinth," in *Christian
      History and Interpretation*, pp. 313–35)
   Brief E: II 2:14—6:2 *(Zwischenbrief)*
   Brief F: I 9:1–18 and II 6:3–13 and 7:2–4
   Brief G: II 10:1—13:13 *(Tränenbrief)*
   Brief H: II 9:1–15 *(Kollektenbrief)*
   Brief I: II 1:1—2:13 and 7:5–8:24 *(Freudenbrief)*

86 Barth, *Resurrection of the Dead*, pp. 13–124.

87 Ernst Käsemann, *Der Ruf der Freiheit*, p. 86.

88 William Wrede, *Paul*, pp. 105–6, 111.

89 Cf. the temporal clauses in 1 Corinthians 15: *epeita* (v. 23); *eita* (v. 24); *tagma* (v. 23); *achri hou* (v. 25); *tote* (vv. 28, 54, 58); *prōton epeita* (v. 46); the future tenses in vv. 49–55.

90   Schweitzer, *Mysticism of Paul;* Werner, *Die Entstehung des christli-chen Dogmas;* Fritz Buri, *Die Bedeutung der neutestamentlichen Eschatologie.*
91   Cullmann, *Christ and Time,* p. 139.
92   Werner, *Die Entstehung des christlichen Dogmas.*
93   Lars Hartman, "Functions of Some So-Called Apocalyptic Timetables."
94   Cf. Aristotle *Physics* 1.14: "Time indeed seems to be like a circle." Cf. also the Hellenistic concept of the "wheel of birth and rebirth" (Origen *Contra Celsum* 4.68).

## Bibliography

Althaus, Paul. *Die letzten Dinge: Lehrbuch der Eschatologie.* 7th ed. Gütersloh: C. Bertelsmann, 1957.

Aristotle. *Physics.*

Barth, Karl. *The Resurrection of the Dead.* New York: Fleming H. Revell, 1933.

———. *Der Römerbrief* 3d ed. Munich: C. Kaiser, 1924. English translation (from the 6th German ed.): *The Epistle to the Romans.* London: Oxford University, 1933.

Bauer, Walter. *Das Leben Jesu im Zeitalter der neutestamentlichen Apokryphen.* Tübingen: J. C. B. Mohr (Paul Siebeck), 1909.

Baumgarten, Jörg. *Paulus und die Apokalyptik: Die Auslegung apokalyptischer Überlieferungen in den echten Paulusbriefen.* Neukirchen-Vluyn: Neukirchener, 1975.

Becker, Jürgen. *Das Heil Gottes.* Studien zur Umwelt des Neuen Testaments 3. Göttingen: Vandenhoeck & Ruprecht, 1964.

Bertram, George. "Die Himmelfahrt Jesu vom Kreuz aus und der Glaube an seine Auferstehung." In *Festgabe für Adolf Deissmann zum 60. Geburtstag, 7. November 1926.* Tübingen: J. C. B. Mohr (Paul Siebeck), 1927. Pp. 187–217.

Bousset, Wilhelm. *Die Religion des Judentums im späthellenistischen Zeitalter.* 3d ed. by H. Gressmann. Tübingen: J. C. B. Mohr (Paul Siebeck), 1926.

Bultmann, Rudolf Karl. *"Elpis."* In *Theological Dictionary of the New Testament.* Edited by G. Kittel and G. Friedrich. 9 vols. Grand Rapids: Wm. B. Eerdmans, 1964–74. Vol. 2, pp. 517–23, 529–35.

———. "New Testament and Mythology." In *Kerygma and Myth* 1. Edited by H. W. Bartsch. London: S.P.C.K., 1953. Pp. 1–44.

———. *Primitive Christianity in Its Contemporary Setting*. New York: Meridian Books, 1956. Reprinted 1980 by Fortress Press, Philadelphia.

———. *Theology of the New Testament*. 2 vols. New York: Charles Scribner's Sons, 1951–55.

Conzelmann, Hans Georg. "Zur Analyse der Bekenntnisformel I. Kor. 15,3–5." *Evangelische Theologie* 25 (1965): 1–11. English translation: "On the Analysis of the Confessional Formula in I Corinthians 15:3–5." *Interpretation* 20 (1966): 15–25.

Cross, Frank Moore. *The Ancient Library of Qumran and Modern Biblical Studies*. London: G. Duckworth, 1958.

Cullmann, Oscar. *Christ and Time: The Primitive Christian Conception of Time and History*. Philadelphia: Westminster Press, 1950.

Davies, William David. "The Jewish Background of the Teaching of Jesus: Apocalyptic and Pharisaism." In *Christian Origins and Judaism*. Philadelphia: Westminster Press, 1962. Pp. 19–30.

———. *Paul and Rabbinic Judaism: Some Rabbinic Elements in Pauline Theology*. 4th ed. Philadelphia: Fortress Press, 1980. London: S.P.C.K., 1981.

Dodd, Charles Harold. *New Testament Studies*. New York: Charles Scribner's Sons, 1954.

Dodds, Eric Robertson. *Pagan and Christian in an Age of Anxiety: Some Aspects of Religious Experience from Marcus Aurelius to Constantine*. Cambridge: At the University, 1965.

Duhm, Bernhard. *Israels Propheten*. 2d ed. Tübingen: J. C. B. Mohr (Paul Siebeck), 1922.

Friedrich, Gerhard. "1. Thessalonicher 5,1–11, der apologetische Einschub eines Späteren." In *Auf das Wort kommt es an: Gesammelte Aufsätze*. Edited by Johannes H. Friedrich. Göttingen: Vandenhoeck & Ruprecht, 1978. Pp. 251–78.

Fuchs, Ernst. "Über die Aufgabe einer christlichen Theologie: Zum Aufsatz Ernst Käsemanns über 'Die Anfänge christlicher Theologie.'" *Zeitschrift für Theologie und Kirche* 58 (1961): 245–67.

Gager, John Goodrich. "Functional Diversity in Paul's Use of End-Time Language." *Journal of Biblical Literature* 89 (1970): 325–37.

Ginsburg, Louis. "Some Observations on the Attitude of the Synagogue towards the Apocalyptic-Eschatological Writings." *Journal of Biblical Literature* 41 (1922): 115–36.

Goppelt, Leonhard. "Apokalyptik und Typologie bei Paulus." *Theologische Literaturzeitung* 89 (1964): 321–44.

Hanson, Paul David. *The Dawn of Apocalyptic.* Philadelphia: Fortress Press, 1975.

Hartman, Lars. "The Functions of Some So-Called Apocalyptic Timetables." *New Testament Studies* 22 (1976): 1–14.

Hunter, Archibald Macbride. *Interpreting Paul's Gospel.* Philadelphia: Westminster Press, 1955.

Jeremias, Joachim. "'Flesh and Blood Cannot Inherit the Kingdom of God.'" *New Testament Studies* 2 (1956): 151–59.

Josephus, Flavius. *The Jewish War.*

Käsemann, Ernst. "The Beginnings of Christian Theology." In *New Testament Questions of Today.* Philadelphia: Fortress Press, 1969. Pp. 82–107.

———. "On Paul's Anthropology." In *Perspectives on Paul.* Philadelphia: Fortress Press, 1971. Pp. 1–31.

———. "On the Subject of Primitive Christian Apocalyptic." In *New Testament Questions of Today.* Philadelphia: Fortress Press, 1969. Pp. 108–37. Also translated in *Journal for Theology and the Church* 6 (1969): 99–133.

———. *Der Ruf der Freiheit.* 3d ed. Tübingen: J. C. B. Mohr (Paul Siebeck), 1968.

Koch, Klaus. *The Rediscovery of Apocalyptic: A Polemical Work on a Neglected Area of Biblical Studies and Its Damaging Effects on Theology and Philosophy.* Studies in Biblical Theology 2/22. London: SCM Press, 1972.

Kretschmar, Georg. "Auferstehung des Fleisches." In *Leben Angesicht des Todes Helmut Thielicke zum 60. Geburtstag.* Tübingen: J. C. B. Mohr (Paul Siebeck), pp. 101–37.

Kuhn, Heinz-Wolfgang. *Enderwartung und gegenwärtiges Heil: Untersuchungen zu den Gemeindeliedern von Qumran mit einem Anhang überEschatologie und Gegenwart in der Verkündigung Jesu.* Studien zur Umwelt des Neuen Testaments 4. Göttingen: Vandenhoeck & Ruprecht, 1966.

Lagarde, Paul Anton de. *Deutsche Schriften.* 5th ed. Göttingen: Dieterich, 1920.

Lindemann, Andreas. "Zum Abfassungszweck des Zweiten Thessalonicherbriefes." *Zeitschrift für die neutestamentliche Wissenschaft* 68 (1977): 35–47.

Luz, Ulrich. "Der alte und der neue Bund bei Paulus und im Hebräerbrief." *Evangelische Theologie* 27 (1967): 318–36.

Marxsen, Willi. *Introduction to the New Testament: An Approach to Its Problems.* Oxford: Blackwell, 1968.

Moltmann, Jürgen. *Theology of Hope: On the Ground and the Implications of a Christian Eschatology.* New York: Harper & Row, 1967.

Moore, George Foot. *Judaism in the First Centuries of the Christian Era: The Age of the Tannaim.* 3 vols. Cambridge: Harvard University, 1927–30.

Morgan, William. *The Religion and Theology of Paul.* Edinburgh: T & T Clark, 1917.

Murray, George. *Five Stages of Greek Religion.* 3d ed. Boston: Beacon Press, 1955.

Origen. *Contra Celsum.*

Osten-Sachen, Peter von der. "Gottes Treue bis zur Parusie: Formgeschichtliche Beobachtungen zu 1 Kor l,7b–9." *Zeitschrift für die neutestamentliche Wissenschaft* 68 (1977): 176–99.

Pagels, Elaine Hiesey. *The Gnostic Paul: Gnostic Exegesis of the Pauline Letters.* Philadelphia: Fortress Press, 1975.

Pannenberg, Wolfhart. *Jesus—God and Man.* 2d ed. Philadelphia: Westminster Press, 1977.

Ricoeur, Paul. "Préface à Bultmann." *Le Conflict des Interprétations: Essais d'herméneutique.* Paris: Éditions du Seuil, 1969. Pp. 373–92. English translation: "Preface to Bultmann" in *The Conflict of Interpretations: Essays on Hermeneutics.* Edited by Don Ihde. Evanston: Northwestern University Press, 1974. Also translated in *Essays on Biblical Interpretation.* Edited by Lewis S. Mudge. Philadelphia: Fortress Press, 1980.

Rössler, Dietrich. *Gesetz und Geschichte: Untersuchungen zur Theologie der jüdischen Apokalyptik und der pharisäischen Orthodoxie.* Neukirchen: Kreis Moers, 1960.

Sanders, Ed Parish. *Paul and Palestinian Judaism: A Comparison of Patterns of Religion.* Philadelphia: Fortress Press, 1977.

## (ii)  A Literary Form and a Linguistic Convention

We meet apocalyptic writing all over the place in the second-temple period, not only in Judaism but in other ancient Mediterranean and Near Eastern religions, including Christianity.[2] When applied to literature, the word usually denotes a particular *form*, that of the reported vision and (sometimes) its interpretation. Claims are made for these visions: they are divine revelations, disclosing (hence 'apocalyptic', from the Greek for 'revelation' or 'disclosure') states of affairs not ordinarily made known to humans.[3] Sometimes these visions concern the progress of history, more specifically, the history of Israel; sometimes they focus on otherworldly journeys; sometimes they combine both. I give two examples, chosen more or less at random, beginning with a description of a vision put into the mouth of the patriarch Abraham:

> *We came to God's mountain, glorious Horeb. And I said*
> *to the angel, 'Singer of the Eternal One, behold I have no*
> *sacrifice with me, nor do I know a place for an altar on the*
> *mountain, so how shall I make the sacrifice?' And he said,*
> *'Look behind you.' And I looked behind me. And behold all*
> *the prescribed sacrifices were following us . . . and he said to*
> *me, 'Slaughter all these . . . the turtledove and the pigeon you*
> *will give to me, for I will ascend on the wings of the birds to*
> *show you [what] is in the heavens, on the earth and in the*
> *sea, in the abyss, and in the lower depths, in the garden of*
> *Eden and in its rivers, in the fullness of the universe. And you*
> *will see its circles in all.'[4]*

'To show you what is in the heavens, on the earth . . . [and] in the fullness of the universe.' There is the essence of apocalyptic: to Abraham are revealed secrets of all sorts. As a result, he learns new ways of worshipping the true god, and finally glimpses (chapter 31) the future deliverance of Israel.

A second example is ascribed to Baruch, the secretary of Jeremiah:

*And when I had said this, I fell asleep at that place and saw
a vision in the night. And behold there was a forest with
trees that was planted on the plain and surrounded by high
mountains and rugged rocks. And the forest occupied much
space. And behold, over against it a vine arose, and from
under it a fountain ran peacefully . . . And that fountain
came to the forest and changed into great waves, and those
waves submerged the forest and suddenly uprooted the entire
forest and overthrew all the mountains which surrounded it.
And the height of the forest became low, and that top of the
mountains became low. And that fountain became so strong
that it left nothing of the great forest except one cedar. When
it had also cast that one down, it destroyed the entire forest
and uprooted it so that nothing was left of it, and its place
was not even known anymore. Then that vine arrived with
the fountain in peace and in great tranquillity and arrived
at a place which was not far away from the cedar, and they
brought to him that cedar which had been cast down . . . and
after these things I saw that the cedar was burning and the
vine growing, while it and all around it became a valley full
of unfading flowers. And I awoke and arose.*[5]

Baruch then prays for understanding, and is given an interpretation: a
wicked kingdom (the forest, of which one cedar is left) will be judged,
and replaced by the messianic kingdom ('the dominion of my Anointed
One which is like the fountain and the vine', 39.7), which 'will last for
ever until the world of corruption has ended and until the times which
have been mentioned before have been fulfilled' (40.3).

These two examples are reasonably typical of the literary form.
In the first case, the seer is invited by the angel to view a wide range
of things normally hidden, including secrets of the heavens and the
earth, the beginning and the end of things. This will lead him to a full
understanding and worship of the one god. It also points forward to
the deliverance which Abraham's family, Israel, can expect at the last.

In the second case, the vision is more specific, relating to a particular historical setting. It assures the faithful that the kingdom which is presently oppressing them will be overthrown, and Israel restored. These two extracts are reasonably typical of the regular content, as well as the form, of the apocalyptic genre.

How then, at the level of literary sensitivity, should such works be read?[6] Clearly, with an eye to the symbolic and many-layered texture of the language used. Baruch's vision of the coming fountain and vine owes a great deal to biblical imagery, and already awakens echoes of previous visions and prayers about the plight of Israel and her coming redemption.[7] The rich imagery of the prophets is revived in a somewhat more stylized form but with very similar intent. The writer of *2 Baruch* was clearly not writing, in the last analysis, about forestry and viticulture: living after the disaster of AD 70, he intended to say something about Israel, her oppression and her future hope. But the forests and plants are not irrelevant. They enable him to do (at least) two things over and above straight socio-religious discourse: to awaken the echoes of earlier biblical prophecy for hearers whose minds were attuned to such things, and to cast his message of patient hope into a form which lent it divine authority. Earlier prophets might say 'thus saith YHWH'; *2 Baruch* describes a god-given vision and interpretation, putting it in the mouth of a hero of several centuries before. The intended effect is much the same. The different layers of meaning in vision-literature of this type thus demand to be heard in their full polyphony, not flattened out into a single level of meaning. If this had been noted a century ago, biblical scholarship could have been spared many false trails. Apocalyptic language uses complex and highly coloured metaphors in order to describe one event in terms of another, thus bringing out the perceived 'meaning' of the first.[8]

We do this all the time ourselves. I have often pointed out to students that to describe the fall of the Berlin Wall, as one well might, as an 'earth-shattering event' might perhaps lead some future historian, writing in the *Martian Journal of Early European Studies*, to hypothesize that an earthquake had caused the collapse of the Wall, leading to both sides realizing they could live together after all. A good many readings of apocalyptic literature in our own century operate on about that level of misunderstanding.

Or take another example. Five people are describing the same event. One says 'I was aware of a blur of colour and a sudden loud noise.' The next says 'I saw and heard a vehicle driving noisily down the road.' The next says 'I saw an ambulance on its way to hospital.' The fourth says 'I have just witnessed a tragedy.' The fifth says 'This is the end of the world for me.' The same event gives rise to five true statements, with each successive one having more 'meaning' than the one before. A biblical example of a similar phenomenon occurs in 2 Samuel 18.29–33. David is waiting for news of his troops in the battle against his rebel son Absalom. The first messenger says 'I saw a great tumult, but I do not know what it was'. The second says 'May the enemies of my lord the king, and all who rise up to do you harm, be like that young man.' Both have described the same event; the second has invested it with its meaning. Not only, however, has he said what it was that David needed to hear, that Absalom is dead: he has also invested *that* news with the further comment, that he himself is a loyal subject of the king. Perhaps he knew David's penchant for anger against those who brought good but upsetting news (2 Samuel 1.11–16), and chose to give his message obliquely, couching it as an expression of loyalty. David, in turn, makes his own statement about the same event: 'O my son Absalom, my son, my son Absalom! Would I had died instead of you, O Absalom, my son, my son!' Each of the speakers is referring to the same event. The different modes of speech *invest* the reality referred to with increasing layers of meaning.

Statements about events are regularly invested in this way with all kinds of nuances and overtones, designed to bring out the significance and meaning of the events, to help people see them from the inside as well as the outside. In a culture where events concerning Israel were believed to concern the creator god as well, language had to be found which could *both* refer to events within Israel's history *and* invest them with the full significance which, within that worldview, they possessed. One such language, in our period, was apocalyptic.

More specifically, different manners of speaking were available to those who wished to write or talk of the coming day when the covenant god would act to rescue his people. Metaphors from the exodus would come readily to mind; and, since the exodus had long been associated with the act of creation itself,[9] metaphors from creation would likewise be appropriate. The sun would be turned to darkness, the moon to blood.[10] This is to say: when the covenant god acts, it will be an event (however 'this-worldly' by post-enlightenment standards, and however describable by secular historians) of cosmic significance. Once more, we can only understand this if we bear in mind what I discussed in chapter 9 of my *New Testament and the People of God*: Israel believed that the god who had chosen to dwell on the hill called Zion was none other than the creator of the universe, and that the holy land was intended to be the new Eden. Within the context of creational and covenantal monotheism, apocalyptic language makes excellent sense. Indeed, it is not easy to see what better language-system could have been chosen to articulate Israel's hope and invest it with its full perceived significance.

We must not imagine that all 'apocalyptic' writings necessarily carried the same or even parallel layers of meaning. Quite the opposite is the case. In my earlier example, from the Apocalypse of Abraham, a great many of the things that Abraham is to be shown in his vision are (what we would call) supernatural or transcendent realities, whose only obvious link to the space-time world is that in some cases they concern the fate of those now long dead. Some of the visions are taken up with the glory of the heavenly realm itself. So far as we can tell, much of this is intended to be taken 'literally', that is, as straightforward description of heavenly reality.[11] So, too, it is possible and even likely that a book such as 4 Ezra, written like *2 Baruch* after the destruction of the Temple in AD 70, contains actual visions seen during actual mystical experience, and *at the same time* regularly intends to speak of actual Israel, her present suffering and her future hope.[12] The metaphorical language of apocalyptic invests history with theological meaning; sometimes, this metaphor may be intended by its authors to pierce the veil between heaven and earth and speak directly of the further side itself.

It is vital for our entire perception of the worldview of first-century Jews, including particularly the early Christians, that we see what follows from all this. When they used what we might call cosmic imagery to describe the coming new age, such language cannot be read in a crassly literalistic way without doing it great violence. The restoration which would be brought about was, of course, painted in glowing and highly metaphorical colours. Writers borrowed all the appropriate imagery they could to show the immense significance with which the coming historical events would be charged. How else could they give voice to the full meaning of what was to take place? If even a pragmatic British Prime Minister could admit to thinking of his political mission in terms of Moses leading the children of Israel to freedom,[13] it is no wonder if the historical children of Israel should use exodus- and creation-imagery to express their hope for a freedom that would be in somewhat more obvious continuity with such historical memories.

The cash-value of such language is, admittedly, often hard to determine precisely, and this indeed has been a matter of great debate this century.[14] Of great influence here has been the view of Albert Schweitzer, that Jews of the first century expected the physical world to be brought to an end.[15] Schweitzer envisaged this event as being a common Jewish expectation, involving the arrival on earth of a divine messianic figure. This has been commonly referred to, in language borrowed from a few early Christian sources, as the 'parousia', though the word does not belong in this sense in the early Jewish writings upon which Schweitzer based his theories. This hypothetical event was, so Schweitzer and his followers thought, regularly denoted by language about the coming kingdom of god.

I have come to the view that the critique of Schweitzer launched by Caird, Glasson, Borg and others is on target.[16] Sometimes, no doubt, extraordinary natural phenomena were both expected, witnessed and interpreted within a grid of belief which enabled some to see them as signs and portents. No doubt eclipses, earthquakes, meteorites and other natural phenomena were regarded as part of the way in which strange socio-political events announced themselves. The universe was, after all, regarded as an interconnected whole (which is not the same thing as a closed continuum). But the events, including the ones that were expected to come as the climax of YHWH's restoration of Israel, remained within (what we think of as) the this-worldly ambit. The 'kingdom of god' has nothing to do with the world itself coming to an end. That makes no sense either of the basic Jewish worldview or of the texts in which the Jewish hope is expressed. It was after all the Stoics, not the first-century Jews, who characteristically believed that the world would be dissolved in fire. (This has the amusing corollary that scholars have thought of such an expectation as a Jewish oddity which the church grew out of as it left Judaism behind, whereas in fact it seems to be a pagan oddity that the church grew into as it left Judaism behind—and which, perhaps, some Jews moved towards as they despaired of the old national hope and turned towards inner or mystical hope instead.[17]) Far more important to the first-century Jew than questions of space, time and literal cosmology were the key issues of Temple, Land, and Torah, of race, economy and justice. When Israel's god acted, Jews would be restored to their ancestral rights and would practice their ancestral religion, with the rest of the world looking on in awe, and/or making pilgrimages to Zion, and/or being ground to powder under Jewish feet.

The 'literalist' reading of such language has of course had a profound effect on the study of the New Testament in the present century. If we imagine the majority of first-century Jews, and early Christians, as people who were confidently expecting the space-time universe to come to a full stop, and who were disappointed, we at once create a distance between them and ourselves far greater than that of mere chronology. We know that they were crucially wrong about something they put at the centre of their worldview, and must therefore either abandon any attempt to take them seriously or must construct a hermeneutic which will somehow enable us to salvage something from the wreckage. This was the programme to which Schweitzer and Bultmann—and Käsemann as in some ways the successor of both—gave such energetic attention. In addition, the thought of the space-time world coming to an end belongs closely with the radical dualism which brings together, in a quite unJewish way, three of the dualities discussed in the previous chapter: the distinction between the creator and the world, the distinction between the physical and the non-physical, and the distinction between good and evil. The result is a dualistic belief in the unredeemableness of the present physical world. This meant that 'apocalyptic' could be seen as far closer to Gnosticism than was really warranted by the evidence (see below); that it could be uprooted from its context as part of Israel's national expectation; and that it could thus function as a history-of-religions explanation for (say) Pauline theology, in a way which allowed quite a bit of the previous theory, that of derivation from Gnosticism, to remain in place.[18] That is why, no doubt, an insistence on the 'imminent expectation' of the end of the space-time world plays a vital and non-negotiable part in some such readings of the New Testament.[19]

There is, I suggest, no good evidence to suggest anything so extraordinary as the view which Schweitzer and his followers espoused. As good creational monotheists, mainline Jews were not hoping to escape from the present universe into some Platonic realm of eternal bliss enjoyed by disembodied souls after the end of the space-time universe. If they died in the fight for the restoration of Israel, they hoped not to 'go to heaven', or at least not permanently, but to be raised to new bodies when the kingdom came, since they would of course need new bodies to enjoy the very much this-worldly *shalom*, peace and prosperity that was in store.[20]

Within the literary form of standard apocalyptic writings, then, we have found a linguistic convention, which traces its roots without difficulty back to classical prophecy: complex, many-layered and often biblical imagery is used and re-used to invest the space-time events of Israel's past, present and future with their full theological significance. We shall continue to explore this in the rest of the essay.

### (iii) The Contexts of Apocalyptic

There are three particular points that grow out of this consideration of the literary and linguistic phenomena we have just observed: the personal, social and historical contexts within which such writing came to birth and flourished.

First, the *personal*. One of the hardest questions about apocalyptic is whether any given writer actually experienced the visions he records, or whether he is simply employing a literary genre as a vivid and dramatic form of writing. Here there is most likely something of a continuum. Faced with the whole Jewish mystical tradition, which includes a well-worn path of meditation on the divine throne-chariot as described in Ezekiel 1, it would be extremely rash to suggest that no Jews of the second-temple period practiced mystical meditation, and extremely arrogant to suggest that if they did they never experienced anything worth writing down. On the contrary, nothing is more probable than that many wise and godly Jews earnestly struggled to come close to Israel's god in prayer and meditation. If at the same time they used, as is again highly likely, techniques such as fasting; and if (as is again highly probable) they had already stocked their minds to overflowing with meditation on Torah, prophets and wisdom writings; then there is every reason to suppose that some of them would have had experiences that they would unhesitatingly have regarded as divinely given visions. Some of them very likely wrote them down; some of these writings are most probably among the early Jewish apocalypses available in recent editions. The only problem is: which ones are they? Which apocalypses reflect this sort of experience, and which ones are 'purely literary' works?

There is no obvious criterion for deciding this question. It must remain a matter of judgment and, as often as not, guesswork. But if, as I have suggested, at least some vision literature originated in actual mystical experiences, it seems very likely also that others, who had not had the same mystical experiences, would employ the genre as a pious fiction, like Bunyan writing *Pilgrim's Progress*:

> *As I walked through the wilderness of this world, I lighted on a certain place where was a den, and laid me down in that place to sleep; and as I slept, I dreamed a dream . . .*

> *Thus I set pen to paper with delight,*
> *And quickly had my thoughts in black and white.*
> *For having now my method by the end,*
> *Still as I pulled, it came . . .*[21]

As Bunyan, so no doubt many writers of ancient apocalypses. 'I had a dream', they said; but what they had was a method. And none the worse for that: many a good argument has been advanced under a figure of speech, for the same reason as the Greeks advanced their crack troops inside a wooden horse. The oblique method may work where direct assault has failed.

We may therefore postulate, with some hope of being on target historically, a continuum of experience that gave rise to the writing of apocalypses. At one end of the scale are the full-blown mystics. At the other are those who write about socio-political events in colourful metaphor. In between, there were most likely pious Jews who, without dramatic visionary experiences, nevertheless wrote from a full and devout belief and longing, in words highly charged with religious emotion. Even Josephus (it would be difficult to imagine somebody in our period with less 'apocalyptic' about him) seems to have believed that

Israel's god was active in the historical events he witnessed. One did not have to be a wild-eyed sectarian, or to have embraced all possible varieties of dualism, to write an apocalypse. Josephus himself could have done so, had he chosen, abandoning his normal style but not his worldview. But it was more likely that the apocalyptic style and genre would be chosen by those who found themselves on the wrong side of history. To understand this, we must move from the personal to the social.

The continuum of possible personal contexts is reflected in the variety of possible *social* contexts. It has often enough, and plausibly enough, been suggested that apocalyptic reflects a context of social deprivation. It is the literature of the powerless (Bunyan wrote his 'dream' in prison). To the extent that the writers may have been recording actual dreams and visions, it is quite possible (though not necessary) to understand their work as reflecting an essentially escapist worldview: things are so bad that the only hope is to leave the present world behind and find one's true home elsewhere. That way lies Gnosticism. Equally, though, those who used apocalyptic language to write about the past, present and future of Israel, whether or not their 'dreams' were real dreams or simply well-honed methods, are best understood in terms of the Trojan Horse. They are appealing to ancient authority, usually by means of pseudonymous authorship (Abraham, Baruch, etc.). They are claiming to have insight into the divine plan that is normally hidden from view; this enables a discontented or rebellious group to steal a march on their opponents, and to fortify themselves in the struggle. They are writing cryptically, using secret codes that may get past the censor ('let the reader understand'). They speak confidently of the great reversal which is to come, reflecting an eschatological though by no means necessarily a cosmological duality, just as politicians through the centuries have spoken of the great change that will take place when they come to power. And, as important as all of these, apocalyptic writers use imagery which makes an appeal on a different level from that of the conscious mind. The closest modern equivalent would be the cunning advertisement, using imagery borrowed from one sphere (e.g. romance) to sell products in another (e.g. clothes). On all counts, apocalyptic can function, and we may suppose was intended to function, as the subversive literature of oppressed groups—whether or not it was inspired by out-and-out mysticism, or by good literary technique.

Moving one stage further outwards, we may therefore suggest a broad *historical* continuum as the widest context of apocalyptic. We may expect to find it where intense longing for a reversal of current ill-fortune merges with intense devotion to the god who revealed secrets to his servants in former times and might be expected to do so again. Apocalyptic, in other words, might be expected to flourish in Israel in the Hasmonean and Roman periods, which is of course where we find a good deal of it. This is not simply a circular argument: we have shown why what we have is what we should expect to have. Equally important, we have shown that apocalyptic does *not* belong simply to a private 'movement', separated off from other groups or movements within second-temple Judaism. Its particular method owes a good deal to the use of imagery in the classical prophets: Amos' plumb-line and Jeremiah's smoking pot are proper (though briefer) antecedents for Baruch's cedar and vine, and Ezekiel's various trees are closer still.[22]

This discussion of the different contexts of apocalyptic raises a further important issue. We happen to possess good modern editions of quite a number of Jewish apocalyptic and other writings from this period. Two thousand years ago, the majority of Jews would not even have heard of half the writings, contemporary with them, with which scholars are now familiar; or, if they had heard of them, they might well have disapproved. Precisely because apocalyptic writing ventured into two dubious areas, mystical speculation and political subversion, many ordinary Jews would have regarded it with suspicion or distaste. As with the Qumran Scrolls, we cannot assume that because we possess a first-century text everyone in the first century possessed it too. The apocalyptic writings do not automatically reveal 'what all

Jews thought'; they provide evidence for possible directions that Jewish thought *could* take, under certain specific circumstances.

A further complication occurs when, despite this proviso, a particular writing was taken up and read by a group different from the one where it was produced. It is quite likely that new readings would result, bearing no doubt a family likeness to the original intention but by no means reproducing it faithfully. When, in addition, such subsequent readings became rewritings, through interpolation, omission, or rearrangement, we find ourselves looking at a canvas on which many artists, and perhaps some heavy-handed restorers, have been at work.[23] Attempting to plot where the writing belongs within a historical framework, then, becomes harder, not easier, as more becomes known about it. These remarks do not indicate that apocalyptic writings are useless in helping us to understand how first-century Jewish minds worked, but they suggest caution in drawing conclusions from them.

### (iv)  On 'Representation'

One of the obvious features of apocalyptic language is the use of symbols and images to represent nations and races. Daniel 7.1–8 speaks of four great beasts that come up out of the sea: nobody imagines the writer to be suggesting that actual fabulous animals would be dragging themselves out of the Mediterranean and climbing up the escarpment, all wet and monstrous, to attack Jerusalem. The sea *represents* evil or chaos, and the beasts *represent* kingdoms and/or kings, as is explained in verse 17. Josephus' interpretation of the parallel vision in chapter 2 suggests that he understood the first beast, the lion, as representing the Babylonian empire.[24] The fourth beast (verses 7–8) clearly represents not simply an individual king, but a whole kingdom, out of which emerge ten 'horns' which represent individual kings (verses 19–26). This sense of 'representation' is common and well known. It is a standard feature of the genre. Jeremiah's smoking pot 'represents' the wrath which will be poured out on Israel. Nathan's 'ewe lamb' *represents* Bathsheba.[25] This is *literary* or *rhetorical* representation: a writer or speaker uses a figure, within a complex metaphor or allegory, to represent a person, a nation, or indeed anything else. In *Pilgrim's Progress*, people in the story *represent* qualities, virtues, temptations, and so forth, in real life.

There is, however, a second sense of 'representation', namely the *sociological* representation whereby a person or group is deemed to represent, to stand in for, to carry the fate or fortunes of, another person or group (the former does not necessarily have to be numerically smaller than the latter, though it usually is: one can imagine a group of people saying 'We have come to represent the Queen'). This has nothing necessarily to do with literary forms or conventions, and everything to do with social and political customs and beliefs. In particular, it has often been pointed out that in the ancient world, as sometimes in the modern, the leaders or rulers of nations 'represent' their people: a good example is the subversively royal act of David, fighting Goliath on behalf of all Israel, after his anointing by Samuel but long before the death of the reigning king, Saul.[26]

There is a third sense of 'representation', which will cause yet more confusion unless it is unearthed and clarified. In the mainline Jewish worldview, according to which the heavenly and the earthly realms are distinct but closely intertwined (instead of either being held apart, as in Epicureanism, or fused into one, as in pantheism), the belief emerges that heavenly beings, often angels, are the counterparts or 'representatives' of earthly beings, often nations or individuals. This *metaphysical* representation is clear in, for instance, Daniel 10.12–21, where the angel Michael is the 'prince' of Israel, fighting against the angelic 'princes' of Persia and Greece. This battle is not to be thought of as essentially different from the one taking place on earth. The language of metaphysical representation is a way of ensuring that the earthly events (puzzling and worrying though they may seem) are in fact bound up with the heavenly dimension, and thus invested both with a significance which may not appear on the surface and with a clear hope for a future that goes beyond what could be predicted from socio-political observation.

Confusion arises here, understandably, because it is perfectly possible to envisage these three quite different senses of 'representation' being used at the same time. Indeed, we have already seen that in the case of Daniel's first three beasts it is not clear whether, at the *literary* level, they represent individual kings or whole kingdoms, whereas with the fourth beast we are left in no doubt (the beast is the kingdom, its horns are the kings). The reason for this unclarity about the first three beasts occurs precisely because a king represents (in the *sociological* sense) the nation over which he rules. Similarly, it would be possible to argue that in Daniel 10 the 'princes' are simply literary devices, 'representatives' in a literary, and not a metaphysical, sense, on the grounds that in chapter 11 there is what seems to be an interpretation of chapter 10, in which the 'princes' are nowhere to be seen, and instead we have simply warring kingdoms. This, I think, would be wrong. There is sufficient evidence of belief in the actual existence of angels, some of whom were entrusted with special responsibility for particular nations, to warrant us in saying that first-century readers would believe in the actual existence of these 'princes' while not believing in the actual existence of the monsters of Daniel 7.2–8. Rather, the language of Daniel 10–11 is to be put on the same level as the language of 2 Kings 6.15–17:[27] what one can normally see is only one part of the total picture.

This examination of 'representation' within apocalyptic literature helps to explain, I think, why the genre is what it is. Because the heavenly and the earthly realm belong closely with one another—which is a way of asserting the presence of the creator god within his creation and in the midst of his people—it makes theological sense to think of penetrating the mysteries of the heavenly realm and emerging with information that would relate to the earthly realm. Granted this *metaphysical* belief, and granted the prophetic penchant for visionary images of various kinds, it is easy to see how a *literary* form could spring up which would sometimes make use of the metaphysical correspondence between the earthly and the heavenly, and sometimes not (the monsters of Daniel 7 were not, I think, supposed to be actual creatures in the supernatural, any more than in the natural, realm). Nor did this equation leave *sociological* representation out of consideration entirely. A king, appointed by the creator god to rule over (and 'represent', sociologically) his covenant people, might come to be regarded as a special locus of heavenly blessing and protection, a special channel or vehicle of the divine provision for the nation's needs.[28]

It is necessary to keep in mind this sometimes bewildering set of possibilities, because otherwise confusion very easily arises. But the main point should be clear. It is normal practice, within the genre of dream- and vision-literature, that a nation, a group, a collective entity should be represented, in the literary sense, by a single figure, be it lion, bear, leopard, city, forest, vine—or even a human figure. In none of these instances is it necessary to suggest that either sociological or metaphysical representation is present. For those, further evidence needs to be forthcoming. Unless it is, the demands of the genre are satisfied by highlighting literary representation alone.

## (v) Daniel 7 and the Son of Man

'Even a human figure': that, of course, is where one of the largest problems lies, and I hope that, by approaching it from this angle, light may be shed on the vexed question of Daniel 7.13–14.[29] Reading the chapter as far as verse 12, there is no problem. The monsters 'represent' (in the literary sense) nations that war against Israel. Why then have critics read the 'son of man' figure, whom the beasts attack but who is finally vindicated, as a reference either to an individual human, or possibly divine, being, or to an angel? Part of the answer is the confusion between the different senses of representation. What we have in this chapter, I suggest, is *literary* representation, whereby a figure in the story—a human figure, surrounded by monsters—functions as a symbol for Israel, just as the monsters function as literary representations of pagan nations. This symbol is obviously pregnant with the meaning of Genesis 2, evoking the idea of the people of God as the true humanity and the pagan nations as the animals.[30] This strongly implies, with all the force of the imagery, that Israel, though beleaguered and battered, is about to be vindicated. To say, off the surface of the text, that either the writer or others reading his work would have thought the text was speaking of a 'son of man' who was a historical individual, and who, as such, 'represented' Israel as a nation in the second, *sociological*, sense, would be simply to confuse categories. Once again this can be seen by analogy with the monsters: nobody imagines that the author of Daniel, or any of his second-temple readers, thought that there would appear on earth actual monsters who would 'represent' the pagan nations much as an MP 'represents' a constituency. If anyone, within the first-century Jewish worldview, were to take the step of treating 'the son of man' as a *sociological* representative as well as a *literary* one—to suggest that the symbol might after all become reality—such a bold move could only be felt as radical and innovatory, new wine bursting old wineskins.[31] And if such a move were made, so that an individual figure within history were held to be in some sense the fulfilment of Daniel 7.13f., any attempt to make the *literary* imagery associated with this 'son of man' into literal *historical* truth—to imagine, for instance, that he should be attacked by monsters from the sea—would be an extreme clash of categories.

Equally, it would be wrong to jump from the *literary* 'representation', whereby the 'son of man' represents Israel within the logic of the vision-genre, to a *metaphysical* representation whereby the 'son of man' becomes a transcendent heavenly being existing in another realm. Any such suggestion (for instance, on the basis that the 'saints of the most high' in verses 18, 25, 27 must refer to angels rather than Israel) must be resisted again on the grounds that it is a confusion of categories. If, once more, anyone were to attempt to combine the metaphysical and literary senses at this point, I suggest that such an idea would be perceived in the world of the first century as a dramatic innovation.

With these distinctions in mind, we may now go further, and suggest a contextual reading of Daniel 7 which shows, I think, the extreme probability that those who read this (very popular) chapter in the first century would have seen its meaning first and foremost in terms of the vindication of Israel after her suffering at the hands of the pagans.[32] It is clearly important to establish, not so much what Daniel 7 might have meant in some previous existence (e.g. to an original visionary or an earlier redactor), but what it will have meant to a first-century Jew. We have noted the cryptic evidence of Josephus, to which we shall return later. We must now look at chapter 7 in its context, in other words, as the logical conclusion of the first half of the book of Daniel.

Daniel 7 has long suffered from being read in isolation from chapters 1–6. True, the book seems in some senses to divide at the end of chapter 6, with the previous material consisting largely of stories about Daniel and his friends, and the following chapters offering increasingly complex eschatological visions. Even this simple division, however, is misleading. Daniel 2 and 4 have a good deal in common with the later visions, and indeed the early chapters continually stress Daniel's skill in knowing and making known hidden mysteries. Chapter 9, though it culminates in an eschatological revelation, consists mainly of a prayer which fits comfortably within the picture of a Jew in exile already drawn in chapters 1–6. In addition, the strange fact that 2.4b—7.28 is in Aramaic suggests that chapter 7 is not to be divorced from chapters 1–6, and indeed hints particularly at a possible link between chapters 2 and 7.[33]

The first six chapters of the book have, indeed, two common themes. First, Jews are invited or incited to compromise their ancestral religion, and refuse to do so. They are tested in some way, proved to be in the right, and exalted. Second, various visions and revelations are granted to the pagan king, and are then interpreted by Daniel. Thus, in chapter 1, we have a mild opening statement of the first theme: the four youths refuse the king's rich (and presumably idolatrous) food, but become healthier than ever, and are given a position of pre-eminence in the royal court. The second theme is introduced in chapter 2, where Daniel's superior wisdom is demonstrated: only he can reveal, and interpret, the king's dream. The dream itself is of a statue made of four different parts, and of a stone which breaks it in pieces and becomes a great mountain. When interpreted, this refers to four kingdoms, which will be ousted by the everlasting kingdom of Israel's god. The content of the vision (the second theme) is the same as the first theme itself. And this content is one with which we are by now very familiar. It is the main story of second-temple Judaism, told and retold in multiple forms throughout our period.[34] These two opening chapters thus serve not merely as an introduction to chapters 1–6 but as a setting of themes for the whole book.

In the third chapter, Daniel's three companions refuse to worship the king's golden image (possibly intended to link with the 'head of gold', representing Nebuchadnezzar, in 2.38), and are thrown into the fiery furnace, whence they are miraculously rescued and given promotion and honour. The same theme is found in inverted form in chapter 4: Nebuchadnezzar has a vision, interpreted by Daniel, in which he is humbled after his great pride, and recognizes the eternal sovereignty of the one god of heaven, whom the reader of course identifies as the god of Daniel. This mutation is then combined with the first theme in chapter 5, when Belshazzar celebrates a pagan feast with the vessels from the Temple in Jerusalem. Daniel interprets the writing on the wall: the one true god is sitting in judgment on the pagan king who has vaunted himself against him. Israel's god is vindicated, and in his vindication Daniel, the Jew called in to explain the writing (5.13f.), is himself vindicated and exalted (5.16, 29).

This sets the scene for chapter 6, in which Daniel, under pressure himself to compromise his monotheism by praying to the king, refuses, and is cast into the den of lions. When the king comes in the morning and discovers Daniel alive, he has him taken up out of the den (6.23), causes his accusers to be killed in his place, and issues a decree, in language obviously reminiscent of 2.44, 4.3, and 4.34, extolling the god of Daniel:

> *for he is the living God,*
> *enduring for ever.*
> *His kingdom shall never be destroyed,*
> *and his dominion has no end. (6.26)*

There should be no doubt about how material such as Daniel 1–6 would be read and understood in second-temple Judaism, particularly in the Syrian and Roman periods. Pagan pressure for Jews to compromise their ancestral religion must be resisted: the kingdoms of the world will finally give way to the everlasting kingdom of the one true god, and when that happens Jews who had held firm will themselves be vindicated. We may cite 2 Maccabees 7 as a close parallel.[35]

This complex of beliefs and expectations, I suggest, provides the natural and obvious context in which chapter 7 is to be understood.[36] Within the second half of the book as a whole, the two themes from the first half are modified but not abandoned. The individual fortunes of Daniel and his companions become the national fortunes of Israel; and it is Daniel, now, who has the visions, which are interpreted by an angel. Putting chapter 7 in this setting, and reading it as a whole, instead of dismantling it in search of earlier meanings for its hypothetical earlier parts, a consistent picture emerges. The four beasts who come out of the sea (verses 2–8) culminate in the little horn of the fourth beast (verse 8), who makes war with 'the saints' (verse 21). But when the 'most high', the 'Ancient of Days', takes his seat, judgment is given in favour of 'the saints'/'one like a son of man' (verses 13, 18, 22, 27): they are vindicated and exalted, with their enemies being destroyed, and in their vindication their god himself is vindicated:

> *His dominion is an everlasting dominion,*
> *that shall not pass away,*

*and his kingship is one*
*that shall never be destroyed. (7.14)*

We shall come to the details presently. For the moment we must note the more than striking parallel between this sequence of events and the whole preceding train of thought, particularly as it finds expression in chapter 6. Here, as there, the human figure is surrounded by threatening 'beasts'; as we saw, the first beast in 7.4 is like a lion, making the connection with the previous chapter about as explicit as it could be. Here, as there, the king comes in his authority: Darius in chapter 6 acts the part that will be taken by the Ancient of Days in chapter 7. In both, the human figure (Daniel in chapter 6; the 'son of man' in chapter 7) is vindicated and exalted, lifted up out of the reach of the beasts. In both, the one true god is glorified, and the enemies of his people subjugated. Both end with a celebration of the kingdom/ kingship of the one true god. Dramatically, poetically, the sequence is identical. Granted the strong prevalence of exactly this story-line in so much other second-temple literature, it seems to me morally certain that a Jew of the period would have read Daniel 7 in just this way.

There are obvious points of dissimilarity between chapters 6 and 7: Darius is not himself divine; the lions of chapter 6 are not destroyed, but become the destroyers of the actual enemies of Daniel. But these make no difference to the close parallelism. One might almost suggest, in line with our earlier cautious suggestions about the personal and mystical origins of some apocalyptic literature at least, that chapter 7 is exactly the sort of dream—or nightmare—that someone might have if they had been through the harrowing experience of chapter 6, and had reflected on it theologically. No doubt a writer of sufficient subtlety to construct a book like that of Daniel could have made the same connection. Certainly I find it impossible to believe that whoever put Daniel into its final form was innocent of the parallelism.

But is it really legitimate to read chapter 7 in this way? It has become customary to separate out various different elements in it, obscuring the overall effect just sketched. In particular, (a) the 'one like a son of man' has been interpreted as a reference to a transcendent being, or to an angelic figure (or figures), and (b) the various stages of the narrative, particularly the moment of vindication, have been separated out and played off against one another (verses 13f., 18, 22, 27, speaking of 'one like a son of man', then 'saints of the most high', and then 'people of the saints of the most high').[37] Both moves, it seems to me, are in danger of misreading the apocalyptic genre.

(a) Collins is surely right to say that, if the reference is to an angel, that still does not nullify the meaning that the faithful Israelites will be vindicated, since the angel is their heavenly counterpart.[38] But this move, I think, is simply not necessary. Though it is true that in chapter 10 and elsewhere Michael, the 'prince' of Israel, fights against the 'princes' of the pagan nations, this need not stand as a model for the interpretation of chapter 7; nor is the reference to 'the saints' necessarily to be taken to denote angels, despite the possible parallels in Qumran. We have here the confusion outlined above, between apocalyptic metaphor, i.e. *literary* representation, and speculative ontology, i.e. *metaphysical* representation. In the former, a 'vision' is a way of referring to earthly realities while investing them with their theological significance. In the latter, such a vision becomes a literal window on actual 'heavenly' events, important no doubt because they will have their inevitable earthly counterpart, but also attracting attention in and of themselves. There is, to be sure, a short route between these two possible sets of meaning; but the parallels we have seen between chapter 7 and chapters 1–6 encourage me to assert that in chapter 7 at least, whatever may be the case later on, the natural way of reading the vision is to see the 'one like the son of man' as 'representing' (in the literary, not the sociological or metaphysical, sense) the 'people of the saints of the most high'. That is to say, the vision is *about* the suffering of Israel at the hands of the pagans—more especially, of one pagan monarch in particular, presumably Antiochus Epiphanes—and her coming vindication when the one god reveals himself to be her god and destroys her enemies. Otherwise, we would have expected the 'beasts' to be themselves 'princes' of the nations, whereas they too 'represent' the nations in the literary, not the sociological or metaphysical, sense. When Israel's god acts to vindicate his name, his people will be revealed as his true humanity, as a 'human figure' in contrast to the 'beasts'.[39]

(b) It belongs to the apocalyptic genre that the meaning of the vision should be unfolded step by step (if necessary), not that the meaning should actually change from one unfolding to the next. It is thus perfectly proper to allow the fullest, final statement (v. 27) to be determinative for the earlier ones; and the addition of 'people' to 'saints of the most high' at this point can therefore safely be taken as an indication that this was the reference always intended.[40]

It therefore seems to me perfectly justifiable (though of course the above account remains tendentious, since space forbids the full discussion that would in principle be desirable) to read Daniel 7 in the light of the first half of the book, and to suggest that a Jew of the second-temple period would have read it like that too. Faced with pagan persecution, such a Jew would be encouraged to remain faithful while awaiting the great day of victory and vindication, when Israel would be exalted and her enemies defeated, when the covenant god would show himself to be god of all the earth, and would set up the kingdom which would never be destroyed. The later visions in Daniel 8—12, in my opinion, are to be read as developments from this basic position, rather than as themselves determining the meaning of the earlier portions of the book. And if this is so, it is this overall context of meaning, rather than isolated speculation about the figure who appears in 7.13–14, that must form the basis for understanding the multiple reuse of similar language in the first century.

Putting together the argument of the chapter so far, we may observe the irony of one of the standard features of twentieth-century gospel study. Many have read apocalyptic metaphor (the 'coming of the son of man with a cloud') as literal prediction (a human being floating on a real cloud), despite the fact that the rest of Daniel 7 has never been read in this way; and they have then read potentially literal statement (stories about Jesus in the gospels) as metaphor (allegorical or mythical expressions of the church's faith). This, as we will see on another occasion, is simply to misunderstand the genres involved.

### (vi) Apocalyptic, History and 'Dualities'

As we saw in the last chapter, it is often asserted that apocalyptic literature is in some sense dualistic. We must now tease out the senses in which this is true, and the senses in which it is not. To begin with, it is clear that many apocalyptic writings hold an *eschatological duality* between the present age and the age to come. They are not alone in this: rabbinic writings do so, too, and so indeed do many of the biblical prophets ('It shall come to pass in the latter days . . .'). Equally, apocalyptic writings assume the vital distinction between the creator and the creation (*theological/cosmological duality*) and a firm *moral duality* between good and evil. These, too, they share with all mainline Judaism. Some, as we have seen, exemplify a strong *sectarian duality*, and all of necessity partake of an *epistemological duality*. These, too, have their parallels and origins in the Hebrew scriptures as a whole. Finally, many apocalyptic writings have a lot to say about heavenly beings other than the one creator god: that is, they, like some parts of the Hebrew Bible, express a *theological/ontological duality*.

But when apocalyptic writings are called 'dualistic', what is normally being asserted is that they have combined these dualities, which are common to much of Judaism, with one or more of the remaining three sorts. In particular, it is imagined that they envisage a *cosmological dualism* in which the present space-time universe is inherently evil, and so must be destroyed in order that a different and better world may take its place. Sometimes apocalyptic expressions of piety have led scholars to think that an *anthropological dualism* is present, in which the writer or the group regard their physicality as irrelevant and their spirituality as all-important. And sometimes they are supposed to have held a *theological/moral dualism*, regarding themselves as the people of the good god, and the world, or their opponents, as the creation of an equal and opposite bad god.

These distinctions between different types of dualities and dualisms enable us to see that affirming the presence of the first six types in a particular book in no way commits us to affirming the presence of the last three. The first six, being common to a good deal else in Judaism besides apocalyptic, are not therefore among its crucial defining characteristics. The literary form in and of itself has no necessary connection with the last three.

In particular, it is vital to grasp one basic point. The worldview to which many apocalyptic writings give voice is the worldview shared by many other Jewish writings of the period. In so far as they attempt to understand what the creator god, Israel's god, is doing within spacetime history, the writers of apocalypses share that quest with Ben-Sirach and Josephus. The difference between (say) 4 Ezra and Josephus is not that the former believed in a god who acts in history and the latter does not, but (a) that the former believed that the destruction of Jerusalem was a great tragedy which only a major reversal could justify, while the latter took it as a sign that Israel's god had gone over to the Romans, and (b) that the two writers chose different literary forms, commensurate with their different standpoints, to express these beliefs.

So, too, in so far as the apocalyptic writings attempt to go further, and to speak of a great new act which this god will perform on the historical stage, they are in line with (for instance) Isaiah and Ezekiel. If they try to work out in great detail exactly when this will take place, that may mark them out (along with Daniel) as more given to speculation, but does not mean that they believed in a dualistic or deterministic world while Isaiah and Ezekiel believed in free will. To analyse these writings in such a way is to capitulate to a Josephus-like Hellenization of categories. The more oppressed a group perceives itself to be, the more it will want to calculate when liberation will dawn. But that there is a divine plan, which, though often opaque, is working its way out in history and will one day demonstrate the justice of all its

workings—this is believed by the biblical writers, the wisdom literature, the Maccabaean martyrs, the writers of the Scrolls, Josephus, and
almost everyone else one can think of in the period. It is not a sign that
apocalyptic literature has gone out on a limb; merely, that it sometimes
has a different way of expressing itself, a way which can be seen to arise
not least from its particular socio-cultural situation.

The real problem is that much modern reading of these texts
has taken place within a tacitly Deist framework, in which one either
believes (a) in an absent god and a closed space-time continuum or
(b) in a normally absent god who occasionally intervenes and acts in
discontinuity with that space-time continuum. First-century Jews certainly believed that their god, being the creator of the world, could and
did act in ways for which there was no other obvious explanation. But
that he was normally absent, allowing his world and his people to get on
with things under their own steam—if there were Jewish writers who
believed this, I am unaware of them. The puzzle that faced some writers, namely, why their god was not acting as they wished him to, was
solved, as we have seen, in quite other ways, not least through wrestling with the concept of the divine covenant-faithfulness.[41]

It follows from all this that there is no justification for seeing
'apocalyptic' as necessarily speaking of the 'end of the world' in a literally cosmic sense. This modern idea has regularly been fuelled by
the belief that 'apocalyptic' is 'dualistic', in a way which we have now
seen to be unfounded. The great bulk of apocalyptic writing does not
suggest that the space-time universe is evil, and does not look for it
to come to an end. An end to the *present world order*, yes: only such
language, as Jeremiah found, could do justice to the terrible events of
his day.[42] The end of the space-time world, no. The implicit argument
that has dominated scholarship over this last century has claimed that
(a) the hugely figurative language about cosmic catastrophe must be
interpreted literally, and (b) the clear dualities inherent in apocalyptic
indicate a radical dualism which sought the destruction of the present
world altogether.[43] Instead of this, we must insist on a reading which

does justice to the literary nature of the works in question; which sets them firmly in their historical context, in which Jews of most shades of opinion looked for their god to act within continuing history; and which grasps the fundamental Jewish worldview and theology, seeing the present world as the normal and regular sphere of divine actions, whether hidden or revealed. Literature, history and theology combine to suggest strongly that we must read most apocalyptic literature, both Jewish and Christian, as a complex metaphor-system which invests space-time reality with its full, that is, its theological, significance. The results of this remain to be explored below.

## 2. The End of Exile, the Age to Come and the New Covenant

As I have suggested above, the fundamental Jewish hope was for liberation from oppression, for the restoration of the Land, and for the proper rebuilding of the Temple. This complex of expectations was the direct result of believing on the one hand that Israel's god was the king of the world while facing on the other hand the fact of Israel's present desolation. In the later parts of the Hebrew Bible, and in the post-biblical Jewish literature, we regularly find the same combination of themes, which summon up the key symbols of Israel's entire worldview. To speak of Temple or Land is to evoke the image of exile and restoration, and so to cling on to the hope of restoration.[44]

One of the central ways of expressing this hope was the division of time into two eras: the present age and the age to come.[45] The present age was a time when the creator god seemed to be hiding his face; the age to come would see the renewal of the created world. The present age was the time of Israel's misery; in the age to come she would be restored. In the present age wicked men seemed to be flourishing; in the age to come they would receive their just reward. In the present age even Israel was not really keeping Torah perfectly, was not really being YHWH's true humanity; in the age to come all Israel would keep Torah from the heart. Although the 'age to come' is sometimes described as 'the messianic age',[46] it would be misleading to think that all such aspirations centred upon a messianic figure. As we shall see, in the comparatively rare places where Messianism is made explicit, it features as one aspect of the much wider and far more frequent expectation of a great reversal within the space-time world, in which Israel would be vindicated and the world at last set back to rights under its true king, Israel's covenant god. As we saw, the nations would flock to Zion, either to learn about the true god and how to worship him[47]—or to be dashed in pieces like a potter's vessel.[48]

A word is necessary at this point about the meaning of the term 'salvation' in the context of the Jewish expectation. It ought to be clear by now that within the worldview we have described there can be little thought of the rescue of Israel consisting of the end of the space-time universe, and/or of Israel's future enjoyment of a non-physical, 'spiritual' bliss. That would simply contradict creational monotheism, implying that the created order was residually evil, and to be simply destroyed. Even in the wisdom literature, which speaks of the righteous possessing immortal souls (e.g. Wisdom 3.1–4), there is continual concern with the actions of Israel's god *within* history (e.g. 10–19); and the immortal souls of Wisdom 3 are assured, not of a non-physical bliss, but of new responsibilities in a renewed creation: 'In the time of their visitation they will shine forth, and will run like sparks through the stubble. They will govern nations and rule over peoples, and YHWH will reign over them forever' (3.7–8).

Rather, the 'salvation' spoken of in the Jewish sources of this period has to do with rescue from the national enemies, restoration of the national symbols, and a state of *shalom* in which every man will sit under his vine or fig-tree.[49] 'Salvation' encapsulates the entire future hope. If there are Christian redefinitions of the word later on, that is another question. For first-century Jews it could only mean the inauguration of the age to come, liberation from Rome, the restoration of the Temple, and the free enjoyment of their own Land.[50]

As we saw in the last chapter, if this was to happen Israel's god had to deal with her sins. The end of exile, in fact, would be seen as the great sign that this had been accomplished. The promise of forgiveness and that of national restoration were thus linked causally, not by mere coincidence:

> *Sing aloud, O daughter Zion;*
> *shout, O Israel!*
> *Rejoice and exult with all your heart,*
> *O daughter Jerusalem!*
> *YHWH has taken away the judgments against you,*
> *he has turned away your enemies.*
> *The king of Israel, YHWH, is in your midst;*
> *you shall fear disaster no more . . .*
> *I will deal with all your oppressors*
> *at that time.*
> *And I will save the lame*
> *and gather the outcast,*
> *and I will change their shame into praise*
> *and renown in all the earth.*
> *At that time I will bring you home,*
> *at the time when I gather you;*
> *for I will make you renowned and praised*
> *among all the people of the earth,*
> *when I restore your fortunes*
> *before your eyes, says YHWH.*[51]

The means by which this was to be accomplished were variously conceived. In differing ways, sacrifice, suffering, and the experience of exile itself were held to carry redemptive significance.[52]

The age to come, the end of Israel's exile, was therefore seen as the inauguration of a new covenant between Israel and her god. Building on the earlier promises of restoration articulated by Isaiah, Jeremiah, and Ezekiel, the post-exilic and then the post-biblical writings gave varied expression to the belief that their god would soon renew his covenant—or, in the case of the Essenes, that he had done so already. This covenant renewal would not of course be an event different to the one we have been talking about. The *idea* of 'covenant renewal' focused attention on these same events seen *in a particular light*. When Israel finally 'returned from exile', and the Temple was (properly) rebuilt, and reinhabited by its proper occupant—this would be seen as comparable with the making of the covenant on Sinai. It would be the re-betrothal of YHWH and Israel, after their apparent divorce.[53] It would be the real forgiveness of sins; Israel's god would pour out his holy spirit, so that she would be able to keep the Torah properly, from the heart.[54] It would be the 'circumcision of the heart' of which Deuteronomy and Jeremiah had spoken.[55] And, in a phrase pregnant with meaning for both Jews and Christians, it would above all be the 'kingdom of god'. Israel's god would become in reality what he was already believed to be. He would be King of the whole world.

## 3. No King but God

One slogan stands out from the revolutionary dreams of this period. The Fourth Philosophy, Josephus tells us, were 'zealous' in their attempts to get rid of Rome because they believed that there should be 'no King (*hegemon, despotes*) but God'.[56] Nor was this view confined to a fringe group. Those who rebelled against the census did so on these grounds;[57] the teachers who urged the young men to pull down the eagle held the same view;[58] the revolutionaries of 66–70 were fired by the same thought.[59] 'The kingdom of god', historically and theologically considered, is a slogan whose basic meaning is the hope that Israel's god is going to rule Israel (and the whole world), and that Caesar, or Herod, or anyone else of their ilk, is not. It means that Torah will be fulfilled at last, that the Temple will be rebuilt and the Land cleansed. It does not necessarily mean a holy anarchy (though there may have been some who wanted that).[60] Rather, it means that Israel's god will rule her in the way he intends, through properly appointed persons and means. This will certainly mean (from the point of view of the Pharisees, Essenes, and anyone loosely described as Zealots) a change in the high priesthood.[61] In some writings it also means a Messiah, though one of the striking features of the period is how comparatively infrequent, and completely unsystematized, expectations of a royal figure seem to be.[62] But however the slogan is interpreted in detail, it clearly implies a new order in which Israel is vindicated, and then ruled over, by her god—and, by implication, in which the rest of the world is ruled in some way or other, whether for blessing or judgment, through Israel.

How was the new age, the new covenant, to come about? I have discussed in chapter 6 the extent to which political or military revolution was in the air during the first half of the first century. My own view is to a large extent that of Goodman: 'anti-gentile attitudes which originated long before AD 6, perhaps in Maccabaean times, inspired many different groups, permeating the whole Jewish population and varying only in their intensity'.[63] The whole context of the times in general, of the biblical backdrop, of the Maccabaean example, of the uprisings under Herod, of the sporadic anti-Roman violence under the procurators, and of the two subsequent wars which were mounted by (among others) strict and 'zealous' Jews, all indicate that violent revolution against Rome was a very live option at this time, and that it would be supported not only by those out for their own 'non-religious' ends[64] but also by a solid and well-established religious tradition.[65] If Israel's god was going to become King, there were many who were eager to be the kingmakers, by whatever means might prove necessary.

The phrase 'kingdom of god', therefore, which occurs only sporadically in texts of this period, functions, when it occurs, as a crucial shorthand expression for a concept which could be spoken of in a variety of other ways, such as the impossibility of having rulers other than Israel's god, or the divine necessity of reversing the present political situation and re-establishing Israel, Temple, Land and Torah.

This complex concept picks up and joins together the whole social, political, cultural and economic aspiration of the Jews of this period, and invests it with the religious and theological dimension which, of course, it always possessed in mainline Jewish thinking.

The idea of Israel's god becoming King is to be seen within the context of the whole historical expectation of Israel, dependent (in a people fiercely conscious of the importance of their own traditions) on Old Testament expressions of hope for the universal divine rule. Thus, for example:

> *All your works shall give thanks to you, O YHWH,*
> *and all your faithful shall bless you.*
> *They shall speak of the glory of your kingdom,*
> *and tell of your power,*
> *to make known to all people your mighty deeds,*
> *and the glorious splendour of your kingdom.*
> *Your kingdom is an everlasting kingdom,*
> *and your dominion endures throughout all ages.*[66]

> *For YHWH is our judge, YHWH is our ruler,*
> *YHWH is our king; he will save us.*[67]

> *How beautiful upon the mountains*
> *are the feet of the messenger who announces peace,*
> *who brings good news,*
> *who announces salvation,*
> *who says to Zion, 'Your God reigns.'*[68]

These passages, of course, reflect not only the ideas cherished by certain thinkers and writers, but also the liturgy in which the hope was enacted over and over again.

One of the central biblical books which emphasized this theme was of course Daniel—which, significantly, was a favourite of revolutionary-minded Jews in the first century, since they reinterpreted it so that it spoke of a kingdom to be set up against the present Roman oppression.[69] Josephus is a little coy about this precise interpretation, no doubt because of his own Roman patronage, but there can be little doubt how his contemporaries read the book. In *Antiquities* 10.203–10 he describes the dream of Daniel 2.1–45, in which the idolatrous statue is destroyed by the 'stone', but he alters it to avoid making it explicit that the Roman empire is symbolized by the mixture of iron and clay (2.33, 41–3) or suggesting that Rome was to be destroyed by the 'stone'. The obvious inference is drawn by Josephus' modern editor, Ralph Marcus:[70] in first-century interpretation the stone was taken as a prophecy of the messianic kingdom which would destroy the Roman empire.[71] Of particular significance is the passage in *War* 6.312–15, which describes 'an ambiguous oracle' from the Jewish scriptures which 'more than all else incited [the Jews] to the war', proclaiming that 'one from their country would become ruler of the world'. Josephus, of course, interprets this to mean the Emperor Vespasian, who was first proclaimed as such on Jewish soil; but he notes that many 'wise men' believed that it referred to someone of Jewish race, 'until the ruin of their country and their own destruction convicted them of their folly'. Word of this oracle also reached the Roman historians Tacitus and Suetonius, probably independently.[72] Despite Josephus' own reinterpretation, the common first-century view shines through: from the Jews would arise a leader, a great king, who would rule over the whole world, destroying all rival empires.

The point can be made graphically with the help of two texts which we know to have been current in the first century. To begin with, the 'Testament of Moses' puts into the mouth of its hero a 'prophecy' about the corruption and wickedness of the second-temple period, and foretells the coming kingdom in which the pagans will be defeated and Israel vindicated. These very much this-worldly events are to be interpreted as the victory of Israel's god:

*Then his kingdom will appear throughout his whole
 creation.*
*Then the devil will have an end.*
*Yea, sorrow will be led away with him.*

*Then will be filled the hands of the messenger,
 who is in the highest place appointed.*
*Yea, he will at once avenge them of their enemies.*

*For the Heavenly One will arise from his kingly throne.*
*Yea, he will go forth from his holy habitation
 with indignation and wrath on behalf of his sons.*
*And the earth will tremble, even to its ends shall it be
 shaken.*
*And the high mountains will be made low.*
*Yea, they will be shaken, as enclosed valleys they will
 fall.*

*The sun will not give light.*
*And in darkness the horns of the moon will flee.*
*Yea, they will be broken in pieces.*

*It will be turned wholly into blood.*
*Yea, even the circle of the stars will be thrown into
 disarray.*

*And the sea all the way to the abyss will retire,
 to the sources of waters which fail.*
*Yea, the rivers will vanish away.*

*For God the Most High will surge forth,
 the Eternal One alone.*

> *In full view will he come to work vengeance on the*
>      *nations.*
> *Yea, all their idols will he destroy.*
>
> *Then will you be happy, O Israel!*
> *And you will mount up above the necks and wings of*
>      *an eagle.*
> *Yea, all things will be fulfilled.*
>
> *And God will raise you to the heights.*
> *Yea, he will fix you firmly in the heaven of the stars,*
>      *in the place of their habitations.*
>
> *And you will behold from on high.*
> *Yea, you will see your enemies on the earth.*
>
> *And, recognizing them, you will rejoice.*
> *And you will give thanks.*
> *Yea, you will confess your creator.*[73]

It should be clear from the context of this poem that its meaning is not to be found by taking the cosmic imagery 'literally'. Sun, moon and stars function within a poem like this as deliberate symbols for the great powers of the world: to speak of them being shaken or dimmed is the kind of language a first-century writer might use quite naturally to express the awesome significance of great political events, such as the terrifying year (AD 68–9) in which four Roman emperors met violent deaths, and a fifth marched from Palestine to claim the throne. And the vindication of Israel, which is the correlative of Israel's god becoming king, should not be thought of as her translation into a transcendent sphere, removed from the space-time universe: the hope is in direct continuity with the events which precede it, but because it is still (from the writer's point of view) in the future it cannot be described in the same way. The language and imagery of the poem is designed to *denote* future socio-political events, and to *invest* those events with their full 'theological' significance. Israel is to defeat her foes, under the leadership of an appointed 'messenger', perhaps a priest;[74] and *that means* that Israel's god is to become King.

The same point emerges from the vivid passage in the War Scroll which speaks in the same breath of detailed military preparations and plans and of Israel's god becoming king:

> *Then two divisions of foot-soldiers shall advance and shall station themselves between the two formations. The first division shall be armed with a spear and a shield, and the second with a shield and a sword, to bring down the slain by the judgment of God, and to bend the enemy formation by the power of God, to pay the reward of their wickedness to all the nations of vanity. And sovereignty [meluchah, kingship] shall be to the God of Israel, and He shall accomplish mighty deeds by the saints of his people.[75]*

It is clear from this that the detailed military plans are intended to put into effect the coming kingdom: that is, the writer of the Scroll believes that Israel's god will become king by means of the military action he is describing in advance. When Israel wins the victory, *that is to be seen as* the coming of the kingdom of YHWH. The deeds of his 'saints' are not something other than the operation of his mighty deeds; the two are identified. The modern distinction between socio-political events and the 'transcendent' dimension can only be related to the first-century Jewish worldview if we realize that the various different sets of language which were available at the time were used *to denote the same events*.[76]

An example from a very different context shows how widespread this 'kingdom'-language was. In the *Wisdom of Solomon*, hardly a book one would associate with strident revolutionary polemic, the vindication of the righteous ones will be the means of the divine kingship:

*In the time of their visitation they will shine forth,*
*and will run like sparks through the stubble.*
*They will govern nations and rule over peoples,*
*and the Lord will reign over them forever.*[77]

These instances show clearly enough the use of 'kingdom'-language in our period. It was a regular means of expressing the national hope, invoking in its support the belief that Israel's god was the only god—in other words, using Jewish monotheism and covenant theology in the service of eschatology. Israel's god would bring to pass the restoration from exile, the renewal of the covenant. Because he was also the creator god, this event could not adequately be described without the use of cosmic imagery. Israel's victory over the nations, the rebuilding of the Temple, the cleansing of the Land: all these together amounted to nothing short of a new creation, a new Genesis.

To speak of the kingdom of this god does not, therefore, mean that one is slipping into a dualistic mode of thought, or imagining that the event which is to come would be related only marginally or tangentially to space-time events. This kingdom was not a timeless truth, nor an abstract ethical ideal, nor the coming end of the space-time universe. Nor did the phrase itself *denote* a community, though it would *connote* the birth of a new covenant community. It would denote, rather, the action of the covenant god, within Israel's history, to restore her fortunes, to bring to an end the bitter period of exile, and to defeat, through her, the evil that ruled the whole world. This restoration of Israel, celebrated in the regular liturgy, is part of the meaning of her god's becoming king. Israel herself is the people through whom the king will rule.

One false trail must be marked off at this point. There is not much evidence for a direct connection between the symbol 'kingdom of god' and the coming of a Messiah.[78] Those texts that speak of a Messiah can of course be integrated into those that speak of the divine kingdom. The Messiah will fight the battles which will bring in this kingdom. But the apparent tension of YHWH as King and the Messiah as King does not really arise, mainly because the two are not usually spoken of in the same texts. In any case, as we saw, YHWH's being King does not mean that Israel will have no rulers at all, but that she will have the *right* rulers. Neither the Hasmoneans, nor Herod and his family, nor Caiaphas and his relations, nor Caesar himself, will rule Israel and the world. Rather, there will be a line of true priests who will minister before YHWH properly, and teach the people the true Torah; and (perhaps) a King who will be the true Son of David, who will dash the nations in pieces like a potter's vessel, and execute true justice within Israel. These hopes, which we may broadly call 'messianic', remained fragmentary. Where they occurred, this is how they fitted, without difficulty, into the wider and far more important overall expectation of YHWH's coming kingdom. To support this contention we must now look in a little more detail at the hope of a coming Messiah.

## 4. The King That Would Come

Modern scholarship has made one thing quite clear: there was no single, monolithic and uniform 'messianic expectation' among first-century Jews.[79] Most of the Jewish literature we possess from the period has no reference to a Messiah; a good deal of prominent and powerful writing ignores the theme altogether. Such evidence as there is is scattered and diverse, spread across very different writings with a hint here, a dark saying there, and only occasionally a clear statement about a coming Son of David who would execute YHWH's wrath on the Gentiles, or rebuild the Temple, or otherwise fulfil Israel's hopes. Nor can we easily appeal to the rabbis for help here, any more than elsewhere in second-temple Judaism. Their conceptions of a coming Messiah were so coloured by their awareness of the failure of the two great wars that we cannot expect much early historical material to have survived unscathed.[80] So, despite the confident pronouncements of many generations, both Christian and Jewish, we must conclude initially that we cannot say what, if anything, the average Jew-in-the-market-place believed about a coming Messiah. In the surviving literature, 'when an individual Messiah is envisaged, his role and character remain vague and undefined'.[81]

This apparently unpromising start invites an explanation, and three obvious possibilities emerge. First, the idea of a Messiah may have been comparatively unimportant in the period. Second, the literature we happen to have may not be very representative. Third, messianic expectations may have been suppressed in literature composed after the failure of one or other of the would-be messianic movements, or after the rise of Christianity. There may be some truth in all of these suggestions. But at the same time the very diversity and unstandardized nature of the evidence suggests that the idea of a Messiah was at least latent in several varieties of Judaism; that it could be called to consciousness if circumstances demanded; and that there were at least *some* more or less constant factors within the diversity. We must now examine the evidence and see what can be made of it.

We may begin with four fairly solid historical points. First, Josephus informs us of various messianic movements up to and during the war of 66–70, and we know a good deal about the subsequent one under bar-Kochba. I have already told the story of these movements in chapters 6 and 7 of my *New Testament and the People of God*. What matters here is the fact that they existed at all: that, under certain circumstances, reasonably large numbers of Jews would choose a previously unknown man (or, in the case of the Sicarii, a member of a would-be dynasty) and put him forward as a king, giving him a regal diadem and expecting him to lead them in a populist movement towards some kind of revolution. No doubt there are distinctions to be made between these various movements. But all of them bear witness to a reasonably widespread Jewish hope, cherished no doubt among some classes more than others, that there would come a king through whom Israel's god would liberate his people. In at least one case, the movement seems to have taken an explicitly 'Davidic' form.[82] If we knew nothing more than this, we would already know a lot.[83]

Second, we may note the significance of the aspirations apparently cherished by Herod the Great. According to Josephus, Herod undertook the massive project of rebuilding the Temple in a deliberate attempt to imitate, and perhaps outdo, David's son Solomon.[84] As I have shown regarding Temple-ideology in chapter 8 of my *New Testament and the People of God*, he who builds the Temple legitimates himself as king, just as the Maccabaean triumph was able to launch a century-long dynasty not least because Judas Maccabaeus had successfully cleansed the Temple from its pagan pollution. Herod, perhaps realizing that the Jews would never come to accept him as the fulfilment of their hopes, married Mariamne, a Hasmonean princess, probably hoping that, if he had a son by her, that the son would not only complete the rebuilding of the Temple, but would also perpetuate the royal claim of the predecessors whom Herod himself had supplanted. Once again, what matters for our purposes is not that this plan failed, since the Temple was not finally completed until Herod's line had been reduced to insignificance, and since Mariamne and her two elder sons were suspected of treachery and murdered while Herod was still alive; nor that many Jews did not accept the Hasmonean claim, and many more did not accept Herod's either. What matters is that such claims could even be advanced. We may assume that Herod had some idea of how his contemporaries' minds worked. If he was hoping to play on a popular idea of a coming messianic king, then we must assume that such an idea at least existed, even if he was quite able, because of its vagueness, to remould it in his own way.

Third, we may note the significance of the bar-Kochba rebellion. It was clearly a messianic movement, as the solid rabbinic tradition attests, citing Akiba, one of the Mishnah's heroes, as having hailed the unfortunate rebel leader as 'Son of the Star' and Son of David.[85] Again, the details are not important. What matters is that we have here further evidence that throughout the second-temple period messianic ideas *could*, under certain circumstances, be evoked; that ordinary people would know what was being talked about; and that many Jews would instinctively rally to a sufficiently credible messianic claimant.

Fourth, we may note the importance of the New Testament itself within this historical sketch. It has been customary in many scholarly circles to assert that the early church quite soon abandoned Jewish messianic ideas, and referred to Jesus in quite different terms. In the light of the comparative scarcity of such ideas in Judaism itself, however, it is all the more remarkable that not only the title *Christos* but also several clearly messianic themes—Davidic descent, key texts from the Jewish Bible, key themes such as the link with the Temple—still remain even in the gospels, which are commonly thought to date from about a generation after Jesus, and quite likely after the war. My own view is that the scholars here are wrong, misled by a generation that sought to strip Christianity of all things Jewish, and that the early Christians retained the messianic idea in a modified but still quite recognizable form.[86] After all, even Justin Martyr, in the middle of the second century, regarded it as important that Jesus should have been the true Jewish Messiah. But even if these scholars were right—indeed, especially if they were right, and if Christianity did officially give up Messianism as such—then the persistence of messianic themes throughout most of the New Testament is all the more powerful a witness to the fact that, whether or not we have a large amount of first-century Jewish evidence, and whether or not we can recreate a single unified picture of Jewish expectation, such expectation certainly existed. The early Christians seem to have done, in this sense, what Herod had done: they took a vague general idea of the Messiah, and redrew it around a new fixed point, in this case Jesus, thereby giving it precision and direction. It is especially striking that the *Davidic* Messiahship of Jesus should be given such prominence.[87]

These solid historical starting-points give us a more viable framework to begin from than we would have if we simply started with odd references in apocalyptic and other writings. They indicate, moreover, a further solid and undisputable fact. If we know anything about the formation of Jewish belief and expectation in this period we know that it had a good deal to do with the reading of scripture. And the Hebrew Bible, and the Septuagint in which many Jews were accustomed to hear it read, has a good deal to say about a coming king. The promises made to David, and often repeated, come across loud and clear.[88] They are celebrated in the Psalms.[89] Some of the most wonderfully poetic passages in the whole Bible include passages where the idea of a coming deliverer is prominent: we might cite, obviously, Isaiah 9 and 11, 42, and 61. True, it is important not to assume that if we discover a potentially 'messianic' passage in the Hebrew Bible we can deduce that first-century Jews regarded it thus; but it is even more important not to ignore the regular reading and singing of scripture as a major force in forming the total Jewish worldview, messianic expectations included.

This point is highlighted when we look at four types of second-temple sources which speak unambiguously of a Messiah. In each case, the view taken is based foursquare on scripture. We may begin with the Scrolls, and take first the remarkable fragment recovered from Cave IV at Qumran, dated most likely late in the first century BC, which collects key biblical texts and makes them speak with one voice about the coming king. After a detailed exegesis of 2 Samuel 7.10–11, showing that the writer interpreted the sectarian community in terms of the Temple, the text continues (with biblical quotations here emphasized):

> *The Lord declares to you that He will build you a House. I will raise up your seed after you. I will establish the throne of his kingdom [for ever]. I* [will be] *his father and he shall be my son. He is the Branch of David who shall arise with the Interpreter of the Law [to rule] in Zion [at the end] of time. As it is written,* I will raise up the tent of David that is fallen. *That is to say,* the fallen *tent of David* is he who shall arise to save Israel . . .
>
> Why do the nations [rage] and the people meditate [vanity, the kings of the earth] rise up, [and the] princes take counsel together against the Lord and against [His

Messiah]? *Interpreted, this saying concerns [the kings of the*
*nations] who shall [rage against] the elect of Israel in the last*
*days . . .*[90]

Here we see what some Jews at any rate were thinking around the time
of the death of Herod and the birth of Jesus of Nazareth. The Scrolls,
as is well known, envisage not only a royal Messiah but also another
figure, either a teacher (as here, 'the Interpreter of the Law') or a priest
as in the 'Messianic Rule'.[91] But the biblical basis of this picture of the
royal Messiah is clear, and it is further filled out in a passage like the following, from the 'Blessings' Scroll:

> *May the Lord raise you up to everlasting heights, and as*
> *a fortified tower upon a high wall!*
> *[May you smite the peoples] with the might of your*
> *hand and ravage the earth with your*
> *sceptre; may you bring death to the ungodly with the*
> *breath of your lips!*
> *[May he shed upon you the spirit of counsel] and*
> *everlasting might, the spirit of knowledge*
> *and of the fear of God; may righteousness be the*
> *girdle [of your loins] and may your reins*
> *be girdled [with faithfulness]!*
> *May he make your horns of iron and your hooves of*
> *bronze; may you toss like a young bull*
> *[and trample the peoples] like the mire of the streets!*
> *For God has established you as the sceptre. The*
> *rulers . . . [and all the kings of the] nations*
> *shall serve you. He shall strengthen you with His*
> *holy Name and you shall be as a [lion;*
> *and you shall not lie down until you have devoured*
> *the] prey which nought shall deliver . . .*[92]

Here again the biblical basis is clear: allusions to the Psalms (61.2f.), and particularly quotations from Isaiah (11.1–5) and Micah (4.13), are the foundation. This, we may be confident, was how some Jews at least understood some quite prominent passages in their Bible.

Moving on from Qumran, we find a similar picture in a second source, the well-known passage in the Psalms of Solomon:

*See, Lord, and raise up for them their king,*
   *the son of David, to rule over your servant Israel*
   *in the time known to you, O God.*
*Undergird him with the strength to destroy the*
      *unrighteous rulers,*
   *to purge Jerusalem from gentiles*
   *who trample her to destruction;*
   *in wisdom and in righteousness to drive out*
   *the sinners from the inheritance;*
*to smash the arrogance of sinners*
   *like a potter's jar;*
*To shatter all their substance with an iron rod;*
*to destroy the unlawful nations with the word of his*
      *mouth;*
*At his warning the nations will flee from his presence,*
   *and he will condemn sinners by the thoughts of their*
      *hearts.*

*He will gather a holy people*
   *whom he will lead in righteousness . . .*
*There will be no unrighteousness among them in his*
      *days,*
   *for all shall be holy,*
*and their king shall be the Lord Messiah.*[93]

Once again the biblical echoes stand out clearly: Psalms 2, 18, 104 and 101 are all audible, as are Isaiah 42 and other passages. We must be quite clear: here we have evidence that some Jews of the Roman period were reading their Bible with a definite view of a messianic figure, prophesied therein, who would come and deliver them from the Gentiles. If the Psalms of Solomon are Pharisaic, as used to be thought and is still not disproved, this becomes all the more interesting for the complete picture.[94]

We must now consider, as a third source, a passage we have already noted in another connection. In his account of the build-up to the war in 66, Josephus describes various portents and prophecies which presaged the coming devastation. Why, then, he asks, did the Jews carry on down the road to ruin, even despite 'oracles' in the Bible which warned of their ruin? Because of another passage in the Bible:

> *But what more than all else incited them to the war was an*
> *ambiguous oracle, likewise found in their sacred scriptures,*
> *to the effect that at that time one from their country*
> *would become ruler of the world. This they understood to*
> *mean someone of their own race, and many of their wise*
> *men went astray in their interpretation of it. The oracle,*
> *however, in reality signified the sovereignty of Vespasian,*
> *who was proclaimed Emperor on Jewish soil. For all that, it*
> *is impossible for men to escape their fate, even though they*
> *foresee it. Some of these portents, then, the Jews interpreted to*
> *please themselves, others they treated with contempt, until the*
> *ruin of their country and their own destruction convicted*
> *them of their folly.*[95]

If there is one thing I wish Josephus had added to his entire corpus, it is the footnote to this text which would have told us for sure which biblical passage he had in mind. There are, however, significant clues. The passage, clearly, was one which 'the wise men' interpreted this way; and it had to do with chronology ('at that time').[96] The most obvious candidate is the book of Daniel: if we know anything about first-century chronological calculations, we know that Daniel was combed fairly thoroughly for information about eschatological time-sequences, particularly by 'wise' groups of scholars (compare Daniel 12.3). But which bit of Daniel? The most obvious passage in terms of chronological speculation is chapters 8–9, which provide arcane timetables for calculating the restoration of Jerusalem; these reappear in various works of the period. It has been cogently argued that, according to one way of computing the figures involved, the 'seventy weeks of years' mentioned in Daniel 9.24–7 as being the time between the exile, on the one hand, and the rebuilding of Jerusalem and the coming of 'an anointed prince', on the other, would be entering upon their last 'week' in the mid-60s AD. This would help to explain why those who adopted such a chronology, which is basically Pharisaic, would be inclined to support moves towards revolution in that period.[97] But if Daniel 9.24–7 gives the chronological scheme, where does the idea of a 'world ruler'[98] come from? The obvious passage is Daniel 2.35, 44–5: after the four great kingdoms, represented by the statue made of four metals,[99] 'a stone was cut out, not by human hands, and it struck the statue' and broke it in pieces; 'but the stone that struck the statue became a great mountain and filled the whole earth'. When interpreted, this vision indicates that 'in the days of those kings the god of heaven will set up a kingdom that shall never be destroyed, nor shall this kingdom be left to another people. It shall crush all these kingdoms and bring them to an end, and it shall stand forever.'[100] Josephus' retelling of this story in *Antiquities* 10 is interesting for a number of reasons. Not only does he omit to explain what precisely the stone is doing: he changes the text of Daniel 2.29 from 'to you . . . came thoughts of what would be hereafter' to 'when you were anxious about who should *rule the whole world* after you'.[101] Though in one sense this refers to all the kingdoms that are to come, it particularly refers to the last one, that of the stone. It looks as though we have located Josephus' missing footnote: Daniel, the book which not only foretells things but gives a chronology, was being read in the 60s as a prophecy of imminent messianic deliverance, through a combination of its second and ninth chapters.

But if this is so—and it seems to me easily the best explanation on offer of a tricky passage in Josephus—it is hard to believe that the very similar passage in Daniel 7 was not part of the equation also. Two bits of evidence point this way. First, we have already observed the very close parallel between Daniel 2 and Daniel 7: the sequence of four kingdoms, followed by Israel's god setting up a new kingdom which will last for ever, is identical in both. Second, as we shall see presently, it was Daniel 7 that provided the source-material for several other, quite different, first-century messianic speculations. It looks as though some first-century exegetes, combining Daniel 9 (which is explicitly messianic) with Daniel 2 (which can be made so via the figure of the 'stone', which is a messianic term elsewhere),[102] had achieved what we described earlier as a radical new possibility: a messianic, i.e. individu-alized, reading of Daniel 7.13f.

So, then, unless we are to conclude that some groups (those referred to by Josephus) only called on Daniel 2 and 9, and others (represented by such writings as 4 Ezra and 2 Baruch) only made use of Daniel 7, in their messianic speculations—which seems absurd—it is better to reach the following conclusion: that Josephus' cryptic men-tion of a widely believed messianic oracle refers to the book of Daniel in general, and to chapters 2, 7 and 9 in particular. These happen to be the three parts of the book about which, despite his full recounting of many other parts, Josephus remains silent.[103] Arguments from silence are notoriously unreliable; here the silence is eloquent indeed.

From Josephus to the apocalyptic writings of 4 Ezra, 2 Baruch and 1 Enoch seems a long jump, but these books too, as our fourth sec-tion of evidence, demonstrate a biblically based messianic expectation during the first century. In the case of 4 Ezra and 2 Baruch at least, this expectation had survived the ravages of AD 70, and was looking for a deliverance still to come.[104]

We may begin by noting that for most of 4 Ezra the question of Israel's future can be discussed without any detailed mention of a Messiah.[105] Then, in the 'eagle-vision' of chapters 11–12, we discover not only a Messiah, but a Messiah who clearly belongs within a rereading of Daniel 7. 'Ezra' sees a vision of a many-headed and many-winged eagle, whose wings and heads clearly 'represent' (in the literary sense) various kings within dynasties. Then a new creature appears:

> *And I looked, and behold, a creature like a lion was aroused*
> *out of the forest, roaring; and I heard how he uttered a man's*
> *voice to the eagle, and spoke, saying, 'Listen and I will speak*
> *to you. The Most High says to you, "Are you not the one that*
> *remains of the four beasts which I had made to reign in*
> *my world, so that the end of my times might come through*
> *them? You, the fourth that has come, have conquered all the*
> *beasts that have gone before; and you have held sway over*
> *the world with much terror, and over all the earth with*
> *grievous oppression . . . And so your insolence has come up*
> *before the Most High, and your pride to the Mighty One.*
> *And the Most High has looked upon his times, and behold,*
> *they are ended, and his ages are completed! Therefore you will*
> *surely disappear, you eagle, and your terrifying wings, and*
> *your most evil little wings, and your malicious heads,*
> *and your most evil talons, and your whole worthless body,*
> *so that the whole earth, freed from your violence, may be*
> *refreshed and relieved, and may hope for the judgment and*
> *mercy of him who made it. "'*[106]

As usual in the genre, 'Ezra' finds this perplexing, and prays for an interpretation. When it comes, the link with Daniel is made explicit:

> *He said to me, 'This is the interpretation of this vision which*
> *you have seen: The eagle which you saw coming up from the*
> *sea is the fourth kingdom which appeared in a vision to your*

*brother Daniel. But it was not explained to him as I now
explain or have explained it to you. Behold, the days are
coming when a kingdom shall arise on earth, and it shall be
more terrifying than all the kingdoms that have been before
it . . . [there follows a long interpretation of the eagle with its
various wings and heads]. And as for the lion that you saw
rousing up out of the forest and roaring and speaking to the
eagle and reproving him for his unrighteousness, and as for all
his words that you have heard, this is the Messiah [literally,
'anointed one'] whom the Most High has kept until the end
of days, who will arise from the posterity of David, and will
come and speak to them; he will denounce them for their
ungodliness and for their wickedness, and will cast up before
them their contemptuous dealings . . . But he will deliver in
mercy the remnant of my people, those who have been saved
throughout my borders, and he will make them joyful until
the end comes, the day of judgment, of which I spoke to you
at the beginning. This is the dream that you saw, and this is
its interpretation.'*[107]

This passage is remarkable on many counts. First, it exploits the fact
that Daniel's fourth beast is unspecified (the first three are a lion, a
bear and a leopard), and makes it an eagle, which obviously represents
(in the literary sense) the Roman empire, and is facilitated in doing
so because actual images of eagles were used to represent the Roman
empire in the socio-cultural symbolic sense. Second, it is explicit about
offering a new interpretation of Daniel 7. Third, at the point in the
vision where Daniel introduces 'one like a son of man', this vision
introduces 'a lion, [who] uttered a man's voice'. The best explanation of
this seems to be that the 'man's voice' ties the lion to the 'son of man' in
Daniel 7, while the fact of his being a lion, which would be thoroughly
confusing within Daniel 7 itself, is an echo of Davidic Messianism.[108]
Finally, the dénouement of the scene is, on the one hand, judgment on
the eagle (as the dénouement of Daniel 7 is judgment on the fourth

beast) and, on the other, rescue and relief for 'the remnant of my people'.[109] The 'saints of the most high' of Daniel 7.18, 27, which in its original context, as we saw, is the interpretation of 'the one like a son of man' in 7.13, have come into their own. Treating our passage as a rereading of Daniel 7 as a whole, we must say that for 4 Ezra the 'one like a son of man' represents, in the literary sense, the Messiah, who in turn represents, in the sociological sense, the remnant of Israel. And in this rereading it is quite clear what is going on in real-life terms: 'the chief activity that the Messiah performs in both this and the next vision is the destruction of the Roman Empire'.[110] This explicit reuse not only of Daniel 7 but more explicitly of verses 13–14 shows that it ought to be out of the question to discuss the 'son of man' problem on the basis of occurrences of the phrase alone, or without consulting the root meaning of the imagery in Daniel 7 itself.[111]

The final passage in 4 Ezra concerns a 'man who came up from the sea'[112] and who 'flew with the clouds of heaven' (13.3):

> *After this I looked, and behold, an innumerable multitude*
> *of men were gathered together from the four winds of*
> *heaven to make war against the man who came up out of*
> *the sea. And I looked, and behold, he carved out for himself*
> *a great mountain, and flew up upon it . . . [the multitude*
> *approached the man, whereupon] he neither lifted his hand*
> *nor held a spear or any weapon of war, but I saw only how he*
> *sent forth from his mouth as it were a stream of fire, and from*
> *his lips a flaming breath, and from his tongue he shot forth*
> *a storm of sparks . . . [which destroyed the multitude]. After*
> *this I saw the same man come down from the mountain and*
> *call to him another multitude which was peaceable. Then*
> *many people came to him, some of whom were joyful and*
> *some sorrowful . . .*[113]

Once again this vision disturbs 'Ezra', and he asks for the interpretation. The man from the sea, he is told, has been kept by the most high for the appointed time, when he will go forth to execute judgment. Then,

> *when these things come to pass and the signs occur which*
> *I showed you before, then my son will be revealed, whom*
> *you saw as a man coming up from the sea. And when all*
> *nations hear his voice . . . an innumerable multitude shall be*
> *gathered together, as you saw, desiring to come and conquer*
> *him. But he will stand on the top of Mount Zion. And Zion*
> *will come and be made manifest to all people, prepared and*
> *built, as you saw the mountain carved out without hands.*
> *And he, my Son, will reprove the assembled nations . . .*[114]

Once again there are links with Daniel, though this time there is less emphasis on chapter 7 and more on chapter 2, with the difference that whereas in Daniel the stone is carved out and turns into a mountain, here the mountain is carved out and then turns into Zion. The link with Daniel 7 is made largely through the initial mention of the man 'flying with the clouds of heaven', in other words, through one image alone, and not, as in the previous section, through the whole sequence of thought.

Two things need to be said about this passage for our present argument. First, by the end of the first century AD, when this book was written, it was clearly possible to use and reuse the imagery of Daniel in a variety of ways, focused on the coming deliverance for Israel, and representing the coming Deliverer in a variety of literary images. But that Daniel 2 and 7 were used in this way there can be no doubt. Second, as with Daniel itself, so with the writings that reuse it: it is simply a misreading of the apocalyptic genre to imagine that Jews of the period would take the vivid and often surrealistic imagery of such passage as literal predictions of physical events. Anyone who still doubts this should reread the eagle vision of 4 Ezra 11. The question is, what do these literary images represent in the world of space, time and history?

Both of these points relate equally to the apocalypse which is closely parallel to 4 Ezra, i.e. 2 Baruch. In chapters 39–40, as we saw earlier, the Danielic image of four kingdoms is set out, after which the Anointed One will be revealed, and will convict the last of the wicked rulers on Mount Zion, whereupon 'his dominion will last forever until the world of corruption has ended and until the times which have been mentioned before have been fulfilled'.[115] Whether or not this is dependent on 4 Ezra, and hence does not count as a fully independent witness, it is still evidence for yet another way in which Daniel 7 was being read messianically, and combined with other biblical themes clearly taken as messianic prophecies, around the end of the first century AD.

Moving from 4 Ezra and 2 Baruch to *1 Enoch*, not least to the Similitudes (chapters 37–71), means exchanging comparative clarity for comparative puzzlement. This judgment is, of course, highly subjective, but it is important to stress that, despite the long history of scholarly wrestling with the 'son of man' figure in *1 Enoch*, if we are looking for clear reuse of the material in Daniel 7 we will find it much more easily in the passages we have just examined. For our present purposes it is not important to examine the rambling and convoluted details of *1 Enoch*; we need simply note the different use of imagery.[116]

In particular, the second 'Similitude' (chapters 45–57), though clearly based on Daniel 7, does not attempt to retell the story of that chapter as do 4 Ezra and 2 Baruch. Instead, it begins more or less where Daniel 7 leaves off: with the son of man already on the throne before the Ancient of Days, and now turning attention to the details of the judgment and the righteous rule which are the concluding point of Daniel's vision and interpretation.[117] The two figures of the Ancient of Days and the son of man (or the 'Elect One', as in 45.3 and many other passages; or the Messiah, as in e.g. 52.4) are simply the starting-points for the detailed judgment scene which unfolds; they are taken for granted, and do not themselves have a developing role. We must discuss in a subsequent volume the relationship between these passages and the early Christian writings which make use of similar

imagery. For our present purposes it is enough to note that *1 Enoch*
does not introduce and explain the 'son of man' figure, but simply
assumes it.[118] This implies that at whatever stage the Similitudes were
written, the picture we have seen in more detail in Daniel 7, 4 Ezra and
2 Baruch was well enough known to be taken for granted. The four
kingdoms, the great reversal, and the vindication of the elect, could
be assumed. One could then move on to something else, namely the
intricacies of judgment.

This remains the case in the third Similitude (chapters 58–69). In
chapters 62–3 there takes place the judgment scene that is the climax
of the whole section of the book.[119] Once again the Elect One (62.1),
the son of man (62.5–9), is simply revealed. He does not appear after a
sequence of four kingdoms, nor is he exalted after suffering as in Daniel 7.21–2. He is simply demonstrated before the whole world as the
chosen one of the 'Lord of the Spirits', and the result of the judgment
is joy in his presence for some (62.14) and shame for others (63.11).[120]

What we have in *1 Enoch*, then, is a substantial development from
the picture of Daniel 7. We should not imagine this development as
taking place on a unilinear chronological scale: there is no reason at all
why different groups and individuals should not have made their own
variations on a theme, returned to the original for fresh inspiration,
or harked back to earlier interpretations behind current ones.[121] Nor
is there any need to postulate dependence, whether literary or otherwise, between *1 Enoch* on the one hand and 4 Ezra, 2 Baruch and the
gospels on the other. Rather, what we have here is one more strand in
the richly variegated tapestry of first-century Jewish messianic belief
and rereading of scripture. What is more, it is a strand which indicates
that the authors expect the ideas to be well known. A single piece of
literature may thus open up a window on a larger world of potential
discourse.

What have we learned from this survey of four very different types
of evidence—Qumran, the Psalms of Solomon, Josephus and some
apocalyptic writings?[122] We have reinforced the commonly accepted

view, that there was no one fixed view of a Messiah in the period. But we have also seen that generalized and loosely formed messianic themes and ideas were current and well known; that they characteristically drew on and reused well-known biblical passages and motifs; and that, though the language in which they are sometimes couched is heavily symbolic, the referent in many cases is the very this-worldly idea of a ruler or judge who would arise within Israel and who would enact the divine judgment and vengeance on Israel's oppressors.[123] In particular, we have seen that one recurring biblical text was Daniel 7. The controversies about this passage are too varied and complex to be settled here. But if the interpretation of apocalyptic in general and Messianism in particular which I have offered here is anything like on target, then I am led to concur with the judgment of Horbury, in one of the fullest recent articles on the subject:

> *At the beginning of the Christian era, the Davidic hope already constituted a relatively fixed core of messianic expectation, both in Palestine and in the Diaspora. Exegetical interconnections attest that 'the son of man' is likely to have acquired, within its wide range of meaning, definite associations with this hope.*[124]

We may emerge from this discussion with some cautious conclusions about messianic expectations in the first century. These may be stated in a series of theses.

1. Expectation was focused primarily on the nation, not on any particular individual. The hope we explored earlier in this chapter remains fundamental, occurring far more widely than expressions of hope for a Messiah or similar figure. Sometimes, indeed, texts which might be thought to speak of a Messiah are referred to the whole community, a process which is already visible within the Hebrew Bible itself.[125]

2. This expectation could, under certain circumstances, become focused upon a particular individual, either expected imminently or actually present. The circumstances under which this was possible seem to have been threefold: the appearance of an opportunity (such as at the death of Herod); the particular pressure of anti-Jewish action by pagans (such as under Hadrian); and the crescendo of speculation connected with the attempt to work out messianic chronology.

3. When this happened, the generalized expectation of a coming figure can be redrawn in a wide variety of ways to fit the situation or person concerned. Davidic descent can clearly be waived. The idea of two Messiahs is not a contradiction in terms. The particular felt needs of the time can influence the presentation: Herod could hope for his son to be the true king; the Sicarii could put forward Menahem, or the peasants Simon bar Giora.

4. The main task of the Messiah, over and over again, is the liberation of Israel, and her reinstatement as the true people of the creator god. This will often involve military action, which can be seen in terms of judgment as in a lawcourt. It will also involve action in relation to the Jerusalem Temple, which must be cleansed and/or restored and/or rebuilt.

5. It is clear that whenever the Messiah appears, and whoever he turns out to be, he will be the agent of Israel's god. This must be clearly distinguished from any suggestion that he is in himself a transcendent figure, existing in some supernatural mode before making his appearance in space and time. Generations of scholars have discussed Jewish messianic expectation as though this were the main issue. We have now made a survey of many of the key texts without discovering the theme at all. The only place where it appears for certain is *1 Enoch*, and there (in my judgment) the question presses as to which parts of the writing are lurid *literary* representation and which are to

be 'taken literally'—whatever that overworked phrase might mean in this case. Certainly there is no reason to hypothesize any widespread belief that the coming Messiah would be anything other than an ordinary human being called by Israel's god to an extraordinary task.

6. Nor is it the case that the Messiah was expected to suffer. The one or two passages which speak of the death of the Messiah (e.g. 4 Ezra 7.29) seem to envisage simply that the messianic kingdom, being a human institution, to be inaugurated within present world history, will come to an end, to be followed by a yet further 'final age to come'. The traditions we studied earlier which speak of redemptive suffering undergone by some Jews in the course of the struggle (e.g. 2 Maccabees 7) are not applied to the Messiah.[126]

The coming of the King, where it was looked for, would thus be the focal point of the great deliverance. But what would this deliverance actually consist of? Would it be political, or spiritual, or in some sense both?

## 5. The Renewal of the World, of Israel, and of Humans

We have learned in these last few chapters that a good many things often held apart need to be put together again if we are to understand second-temple Judaism. This is nowhere more true than in the study of the Jewish hope. It is no doubt right, if we are to avoid fuzzy thinking, that we should study different aspects and themes as though they were the only ones in the world. But it is then appropriate, if we are to avoid spurious atomism, that we put the newly polished elements back in their proper relation to one another. Jews of the period were hoping for the 'real' return from exile. They were also hoping for a full 'forgiveness of sins'. Those are not two separate things, but two ways of looking at the same thing. They were looking for the covenant god to fulfil his promises, to display his 'righteousness'. That too is simply a different reading of the same basic phenomena. Some were looking for a coming Messiah who would be the agent appointed by their god to accomplish redemption; but the redemption was the same. They were looking for a restored Temple, and for their god to come and dwell within it; that is the largest dimension of all, but it is still a dimension of the same thing. We cannot split any of these off from one another.

If all these beliefs and hopes are to be integrated closely with one another, they must also be integrated with the basic first-century Jewish worldview which we have studied. And the purpose of such worldview study is to help us to understand history: to enable us to see behind the events to the meaning, in the sense explored in Part II of my *New Testament and the People of God*.

Before we can finally draw these threads together, we must face a question which arises not least from the apocalyptic literature we have studied in the present essay. How did this expectation, the longing for a national restoration, fit in, if it did, with the hope for a non-spatio-temporal life after death? How did personal hope fit in with national hope? How did 'spiritual' aspiration cohere with 'political'? And, in the middle of all this, what about the idea of resurrection?

It is clear that some first-century Jews at least had already adopted what may be seen as a Hellenized future expectation, that is, a hope for a non-physical (or 'spiritual') world to which the righteous and blessed would be summoned after death, and a non-physical place of damnation where the wicked would be tormented. There are some texts which use language of this sort. They can by no means be dismissed as simply the projection on to a non-historical screen of expectations that can be reduced to purely historical terms. Nothing is more probable than that, in the confusion of non-standardized second-temple Judaism, all sorts of groups and individuals held all sorts of views about life after death, including some that, from our perspective, seem closer to a Hellenistic idea of a shadowy afterlife than to any thought of resurrection, or indeed of the renewal of the space-time world of creation and history.

Nevertheless, I believe it would be a great mistake to regard a Hellenized expectation as basic, and to place the socio-political hope in a secondary position. We have seen throughout this essay (and throughout Part III of my *New Testament and the People of God*) that much second-temple Judaism made a serious attempt to integrate what post-Enlightenment thought holds apart, the sacred and the secular. We have also seen that it is easy to mistake literary representation (the use of vivid imagery to denote space-time reality and connote its theological significance) for metaphysical representation (whereby a 'spiritual' or 'transcendent' being is the heavenly counterpart of an earthly reality); and that in this confusion it is all too easy to imagine that language which, in a culture other than our own, would be recognized as highly figurative, is flatly literal. Further, we have seen in our study of Josephus that, precisely when he is discussing the beliefs of Jewish groups, he has a penchant for 'translating' out of the hard political meaning of his Jewish contemporaries into a less threatening meaning, more easily assimilable by his cultured pagan readers.

The problem here seems to be that the language can be read as metaphorical *in either direction*. On the one hand, we shall see that Josephus and some of the apocalyptic works *refer* to physical resurrection while using the *language* of immortality, i.e. a non-physical life after death. On the other hand, it can also be suggested that a writer *refers* to immortality while using the *language* of physical resurrection, in order to make the hope more vivid.[127] How can we gain a foothold in an area of which even the large-scale revision of Schürer declares that 'there are so many opinions in Jewish religious thought that it is not feasible to enter into them all at the present time'?[128] The best course seems to be simply to outline the spectrum of ancient opinion (rather than the spectrum of modern opinion about it, which would be tedious indeed), and point up the various options.[129]

We may begin once more on solid ground, and again in the book of Daniel:

*There shall be a time of anguish, such as has never occurred
since nations first came into existence. But at that time your
people shall be delivered, everyone who is found written
in the book.* Many of those who sleep in the dust of the
earth shall awake, some to everlasting life, and some
to shame and contempt. *Those who are wise shall shine
like the brightness of the sky, and those who lead many to
righteousness, like the stars forever and ever.*[130]

The unitalicized sentence of this extract unquestionably refers to physical resurrection, which in this case is of just and unjust alike. We
should note, however, that this is flanked by two other statements.
First, the opening sentence refers to a time of great national anguish,
followed by the great national deliverance. The hope for resurrection
is part and parcel of the hope for national restoration after the 'messianic woes'. Second, the last sentence refers to the luminosity of the
blessed, the 'wise': they will shine like the sky, or like the stars.[131] By
itself, this sentence could easily have been taken to refer to a non-
physical 'heavenly' existence; in its present context, it demands to be
read as a metaphor for the glory which will be enjoyed by those who
are raised to ever-lasting life (which in Hebrew and Greek is 'the life of
the age', i.e. the 'age to come', not simply 'unending life'). It is not clear
whether the earlier statements of similar views in such passages as Isaiah 26.19, Ezekiel 37.1–14, and Hosea 5.15—6.3 were understood in
this literal sense in the pre-Maccabaean period; there, their natural literary meaning is that they invest the future restoration of Israel with its
theological significance. But we can be sure that those who read Daniel
12 in the full sense just described would have reread such earlier passages and found in them confirmation of the view to which they had
come. After all, as we have seen throughout this essay (and throughout
Part III of my *New Testament and the People of God*), the antithesis
which many have imagined between the national and the individual
hope, between the political and the 'spiritual', is an anachronism.[132]

A second firm starting-point is found in 2 Maccabees. In one of
the most grisly passages in the whole of our literature, seven brothers
are being tortured in the vain attempt to make them submit to the
edict of Antiochus Epiphanes. In refusing, many of them explicitly
refer to the coming resurrection in which they will be vindicated and
given back the bodies that are now being torn apart:

> *And when he was at his last breath, he said, 'You accursed*
> *wretch, you dismiss us from this present life, but the King of*
> *the universe will raise us up to an everlasting renewal of life,*
> *because we have died for his laws.'*
>
> *When he was near death, [another] said, 'One cannot*
> *but choose to die at the hands of mortals and to cherish the*
> *hope God gives of being raised again by him. But for you*
> *there will be no resurrection to life!'*
>
> *[The mother] . . . said to them, 'I do not know how you*
> *came into being in my womb. It was not I who gave you life*
> *and breath, nor I who set in order the elements within each*
> *of you. Therefore the Creator of the world, who shaped the*
> *beginning of humankind and devised the origin of all things,*
> *will in his mercy give life and breath back to you again, since*
> *you now forget yourselves for the sake of his laws . . . accept*
> *death, so that in God's mercy I may get you back again along*
> *with your brothers.'*
>
> *[The young man said] . . . 'If our living Lord is angry*
> *for a little while, to rebuke and discipline us, he will again*
> *be reconciled with his own servants . . . for our brothers after*
> *enduring a brief suffering have drunk of everflowing life,*
> *under God's covenant; but you, by the judgment of God,*
> *will receive just punishment for your arrogance. I, like my*
> *brothers, give up body and life for the laws of our ancestors,*
> *appealing to God to show mercy soon to our nation and by*
> *trials and plagues to make you confess that he alone is God,*
> *and through me and my brothers to bring to an end the*

> *wrath of the Almighty that has justly fallen on our whole*
> *nation.'[133]*

This remarkable passage not only demonstrates again the extremely physical nature of the anticipated resurrection. It also shows the close link between this belief and four others. First, those who were assured of resurrection were those who had died for the ancestral laws. Second, the future bodily life will be a gift of the creator of the universe, an act of new creation, not a mere continuation of an immortal soul. Third, the hope could be phrased in more general terms ('they have drunk of everflowing life'), which by itself might have been interpreted in a Hellenistic direction, without detracting from the emphatically physical view expressed throughout the chapter. Fourth, the hope for resurrection is placed fair and square within the national, covenantal expectation, conjoined with the belief that the significance of the martyr's sufferings has to do with their efficacy in bearing the wrath of Israel's god against his sinful people. Here, in a book which we know to have been in circulation in the first century, is a powerful statement of one regular form of the Jewish worldview.

One other comment on 2 Maccabees 7 is in order at this stage. The first-century AD work known as 4 Maccabees was based more or less entirely on 2 Maccabees, and a good deal of 4 Maccabees (chapters 8–17) is taken up with the retelling and expansion of the chapter we have just studied. Yet, in keeping with the aim of the later book, which is the glorification of Reason by historical examples of those who were prepared to suffer rather than abandon this virtuous faculty, the mention of bodily resurrection has been toned down almost completely, in favour of a much more Hellenistic approach. 'For we,' say the young men in 4 Maccabees, 'through this severe suffering and endurance, shall have the prize of virtue and shall be with God, on whose account we suffer' (9.8). 'I', said one, 'lighten my pains by the joys that come from virtue' (9.31); 'See, here is my tongue,' said another; 'cut it off, for in spite of this you will not make our reason speechless' (10.19); and so on.[134] This is an excellent example of what we will find in Josephus: a firmly physical account of resurrection can easily, under the right rhetorical constraints, be 'translated' into a Hellenistic doctrine of the immortal memory of the virtuous dead.[135]

We find exactly this when we put Josephus' own statements side by side. Take, first, the speech which he puts into his own mouth when defending his right not to commit suicide after the fall of Jotapata. Those who lay violent hands on themselves, he declares, go into the darker regions of the nether world, while he himself believes

> *that they who depart this life in accordance with the law of*
> *nature and repay the loan which they received from God,*
> *when He who lent is pleased to reclaim it, win eternal*
> *renown; that their houses and families are secure; that their*
> *souls, remaining spotless and obedient, are allotted the most*
> *holy place in heaven, whence, in the revolution of the ages,*
> *they return to find in chaste bodies a new habitation.[136]*

This is as clear a statement of one mainline Jewish view as we could wish for. The righteous dead are presently in 'heaven', the domain of the creator god; but there is coming a new age, *ha-'olam ha-ba'*, in which the creation will be (not abolished, but) renewed; and the righteous dead will be given new bodies, precisely in order that they may inhabit the renewed earth. 'The revolution of the ages' is not the Stoic doctrine of the fiery consumption and remaking of a phoenix-like world, but the Jewish distinction between the present age and the age to come. We are left in no doubt that the age to come would be a renewed physical, space-time world, and that the righteous dead, at present resting in 'heaven', would return to share its physical life.

Armed with this passage, which Josephus has claimed as his own view, we may note the slight toning-down which has already taken place in the exposition of Jewish belief in the book *Against Apion*. No

mere financial or other prize, Josephus claims with pride, awaits those
who follow our ancestral laws: rather,

> *each individual . . . is firmly persuaded that to those who*
> *observe the laws and, if they must needs die for them,*
> *willingly meet death, God has granted a renewed existence*
> *and in the revolution of the ages the gift of a better life.*[137]

By itself, this passage might have been thought potentially Stoic, or at
least capable of a general Hellenized interpretation. In the light of the
earlier passage, there can be no doubt that here, too, we have the same
belief as in 2 Maccabees.

It is when we turn to Josephus' statements about the beliefs of
the different parties that we would have difficulty, were it not for these
clearer statements. The Pharisees, he says, hold a doctrine of condi-
tional resurrection, while the Sadducees reject it:

> *Every soul, they [the Pharisees] maintain, is imperishable,*
> *but the soul of the good alone passes into another body,*
> *while the souls of the wicked suffer eternal punishment . . .*
> *As for the persistence of the soul after death, penalties in the*
> *underworld, and rewards, they [the Sadducees] will have*
> *none of them.*[138]

Once again, if these passages were all we had, we would still think of
the imperishability of the soul as the main Pharisaic doctrine, rather
than the resurrection of the body. Even though the idea of the soul's
'passing into another body' makes it clear that this is not pure Pla-
tonism (the soul escaping its bodily prison and inheriting disembodied
bliss), the phrase by itself could be interpreted as meaning transmigra-
tion (the soul passing at death into another physical being), as indeed
some modern interpreters have suggested.[139] In the considerably later
parallel passage in the *Antiquities*, this highlighting of the immortal
soul has been taken a large step further:

*They [the Pharisees] believe that souls have power to survive death and that there are rewards and punishments under the earth for those who have led lives of virtue or vice: eternal imprisonment is the lot of evil souls, while the good souls receive an easy passage to a new life. Because of these views they are, as a matter of fact, extremely influential among the townsfolk . . . The Sadducees hold that the soul perishes along with the body.*[140]

Again, if this passage were all we had to go on, we might conclude that Josephus had gone the whole way into a Hellenistic doctrine of the immortality of the soul. The souls go 'under the ground' where they receive rewards or punishments; the mention of an 'easy passage to a new life' could by itself be interpreted simply as the blessed disembodied life of the successful *post mortem* Platonist. But in the context of the earlier extracts we must conclude that the 'passage to a new life' is a hint, here all but obscured by the language about the immortal soul, of the position which is clear elsewhere: upon death, the souls of the righteous go to heaven, or to be with their god, or under the earth—but this is only temporary. A new, embodied life awaits them in the fullness of time.

Josephus clearly knows all about the Hellenistic views of immortal souls shut up in the prison-house of the body, because that is the view he ascribes to the Essenes, labelling it specifically 'the belief of the sons of Greece'.[141] According to the Essenes, he says, righteous souls go to a place of blessedness beyond the ocean, corresponding to the Greek 'isles of the blessed'. How far this was actually true of the Essenes it is hard to say, and it may be that Josephus' account has been considerably distorted here by his desire to present the different groups as Hellenistic philosophical schools.[142] It is interesting, though, that despite the way his descriptions of the Pharisees' doctrines change in the direction of a softening of the hard resurrection belief, he does not ascribe to them the fully-blown Hellenistic view which he is happy to postulate of the Essenes.

The most strikingly Hellenized account of life after death in Josephus is put on the lips of Eleazar, the leader of the Sicarii on Masada. Advocating mass suicide, Eleazar urges his followers to embrace death as that which gives liberation to the soul:

> *Life, not death, is man's misfortune. For it is death which*
> *gives liberty to the soul and permits it to depart to its own*
> *pure abode, there to be free from all calamity; but so long as*
> *it is imprisoned in a mortal body and tainted with all its*
> *miseries, it is, in sober truth, dead, for association with what*
> *is mortal ill befits that which is divine. True, the soul possesses*
> *great capacity, even while incarcerated in the body . . . But it*
> *is not until, freed from the weight that drags it down to earth*
> *and clings about it, the soul is restored to its proper sphere,*
> *that it enjoys a blessed energy and a power untrammelled*
> *on every side, remaining, like God himself, invisible to*
> *human eyes . . . For whatever the soul has touched lives*
> *and flourishes, whatever it abandons withers and dies; so*
> *abundant is her wealth of immortality.*[143]

No Stoic rhetorician could have put it better. That is probably the point. Josephus is almost certainly putting into the mouth of this rebel leader a speech which would endear itself to a respectable Roman audience, to whom the arguments (and the poetic allusions, e.g. to Sophocles)[144] would be quite familiar. It is remarkable that in the following passage Eleazar goes on to speak of sleep as an analogy to death, and instead of drawing the point that those who sleep will wake again (cf. 1 Corinthians 15.20; 1 Thessalonians 4.13–15, etc.), he employs the thoroughly pagan idea that during sleep humans become independent beings, conversing with the deity, ranging the universe, and foretelling the future.[145]

If Josephus describes the Sicarii chieftain Eleazar, almost certainly quite wrongly, as having used language appropriate to paganism and particularly Stoicism, it is interesting, finally, that when he creates another speech about facing death, this time on the lips of those he knows to be Pharisees, he draws back from such an extreme position. The learned doctors who incited the young men to pull down the eagle on the Temple, he says, urged that even if the action should prove hazardous,

> *it was a noble deed to die for the law of one's country; for the*
> *souls of those who came to such an end attained immortality*
> *and an eternally abiding sense of felicity.*[146]

Immortality here is a gift to the virtuous, not an innate property of the soul; it is still immortality, not (apparently) resurrection, but there is no talk of the soul being weighed down by the body. The later account of the same incident puts the point thus: that

> *to those about to die for the preservation and safeguarding*
> *of their fathers' way of life the virtue acquired by them in*
> *death would seem far more advantageous than the pleasure of*
> *living. For by winning eternal fame and glory for themselves*
> *they would be praised by those now living and would*
> *leave the ever-memorable [example of their] lives to future*
> *generations. Moreover, they said, even those who live without*
> *danger cannot escape the misfortune [of death], so that those*
> *who strive for virtue do well to accept their fate with praise*
> *and honour when they depart this life.*[147]

From this passage we would not glean any hint of resurrection, but nor would we have inferred the presence of the Stoic view, that one should simply be prepared to die for the cause of virtue. Because we know on other grounds that the teachers were Pharisees, we are able to see behind the smokescreen of Josephus' apologetic stance. Josephus is

trying to tell his Roman audience that the teachers were urging their
followers to die in a noble cause, much as a good Roman might have
done. What they were actually saying, we may be sure, was this: Die
for the law, and you will receive resurrection when our god vindicates
his people! They might have been reading 2 Maccabees.

Josephus, then, is valuable in this discussion in two ways. First,
on occasion he clearly states a doctrine of bodily resurrection. Second,
he demonstrates equally clearly that such a doctrine could quite easily
be described, for rhetorical reasons, in language which by itself could
easily be taken to refer to the immortality of the soul. We thus see, in
the work of one writer, what we observed above in the transition from
2 Maccabees to 4 Maccabees.

Where on this scale should we put the Psalms of Solomon?

> *The destruction of the sinner is for ever,*
>    *and God will not remember him when he visits the*
>       *righteous.*
> *This is the portion of sinners for ever;*
> *But they that fear the Lord shall rise to life eternal,*
>    *And their life shall be in the light of the Lord, and*
>       *shall come to an end no more.*[148]

R. B. Wright, commenting on this passage, says that it is unclear
whether it refers to the resurrection of the body (rising from the grave)
or the immortality of the spirit (rising to god), or if indeed the author
necessarily distinguished the two.[149] The same question faces the reader
of the Solomonic Psalms 14.10 and 15.13, and indeed the older belief
that these propounded a doctrine of resurrection may have been based
on the belief that they were Pharisaic, rather than the other way round.
It is, however, perhaps asking too much to expect doctrinal precision
from this sort of poetry. The Psalms are quite compatible with the
resurrection belief of 2 Maccabees and the explicit passage in Josephus,
but by themselves they cannot be forced to yield a clear statement.

Whatever we think about the Psalms of Solomon, it is clear from Josephus, the New Testament, and the later rabbinic evidence that the resurrection was one of the principal distinguishing marks of the Pharisees. Or perhaps it would be more accurate to say that it was the *denial* of the resurrection that became one of the chief distinguishing marks of the Sadducees, the arch-opponents of the Pharisees.[150] As we saw earlier, this dispute between Pharisees and Sadducees is not an isolated point of disagreement, but is exactly cognate with their major bone of contention: the Pharisees looked for a great renewal in which the present state of things would be radically altered, while the Sadducees were content with the status quo. To that extent, it is not surprising that Acts depicts the early Christians as being opposed by Sadducees precisely because they were 'announcing the resurrection of the dead by means of Jesus'.[151] This has the stamp of early tradition upon it: in later periods, the name of Jesus would have been the problem, but in the early days of Christianity those in power were more worried about an excited announcement of resurrection, with all the socio-political connotations that might have. This also helps to explain John's story about the chief priests wanting to kill Lazarus after Jesus had raised him from the dead.[152] The early Christian writings bear witness to the same spread of belief in resurrection: speculation that Jesus was John the Baptist raised from the dead is something that the early church is unlikely to have made up, and it could only have arisen in circles where the idea of resurrection was held as a distinct (though not clearly defined) possibility.[153] It seems, in fact, that Sanders' view here is correct: the great majority of Jews of the period believed in some sense or other in the resurrection.[154] Only those who had gone some way towards assimilation, and who therefore adopted a belief in the immortality of the non-physical soul, or those who for socio-political reasons were committed to denying any speculation about a future life, held back.[155]

This widespread belief in resurrection can be seen in a range of apocalyptic texts from roughly the first century BC/AD. The *Life of Adam and Eve*[156] states clearly that the creator god promised to

Adam that he would raise him on the last day, in the general resurrection, with every man of his seed, and envisages the archangel Michael saying to Adam's son Seth that all dead humans are to be buried 'until the day of resurrection', and that the sabbath day is 'a sign of the resurrection'.[157] *1 Enoch* speaks of Sheol and hell giving back their dead, with great rejoicing on the part of the whole of creation;[158] 4 Ezra, of the earth giving up those who 'are asleep in it';[159] the Testament of Judah, of the patriarchs being raised to life, at a time when

> *those who died in sorrow shall be raised in joy;*
> *and those who died in poverty for the Lord's sake shall*
> > *be made rich;*
> *those who died on account of the Lord shall be wakened*
> > *to life.*
> *And the deer of Jacob shall run with gladness;*
> *the eagles of Jacob shall fly with joy;*
> *the impious shall mourn and sinners shall weep,*
> *but all peoples shall glorify the Lord forever.*[160]

In all of these texts, which can scarcely be thought to come from one single sect alone, we see a well-shaped belief. The righteous will rise to life in the age to come, so that they can receive their proper reward. This belief functions within the context of suffering and martyrdom for Israel's god and his law, and hence as an incentive to a more serious keeping of that law and a more zealous maintenance of all that Judaism was and stood for.[161] Thus, as we shall see presently, belief in resurrection, though often thinking particularly of individual human beings and their future life, was not divorced from, but was rather a quintessential part of, the overall belief, hope, and worldview of a major segment of second-temple Judaism.

It is common to suggest that the Wisdom of Solomon speaks of a blessed, but not physical, future. This is usually illustrated by the following passage:

*But the souls of the righteous are in the hand of God,*
*and no torment will ever touch them.*
*In the eyes of the foolish they seemed to have died,*
*and their departure was thought to be a disaster,*
*and their going from us to be their destruction;*
*but they are at peace.*
*For though in the sight of others they were punished,*
*their hope is full of immortality . . .*[162]

I suggest, however, that this quite clearly refers, not to the permanent state of the righteous dead, but to their temporary home. The passage, which we quoted earlier in another connection, continues:

*Like gold in the furnace he tried them*
*and like a sacrificial burnt offering he accepted*
*them.*
*In the time of their visitation they will shine forth,*
*and will run like sparks through the stubble.*
*they will govern nations and rule over peoples,*
*and the Lord will reign over them forever . . .*
*The righteous who have died will condemn the ungodly*
*who are living . . .*
*For [the ungodly] will see the end of the wise,*
*and will not understand what the Lord purposed for*
*them,*
*and for what he kept them safe.*

*[The ungodly] will come with dread when their sins are*
*reckoned up,*
*and their lawless deeds will convict them to their*
*face.*
*Then the righteous will stand with great confidence*
*in the presence of those who have oppressed them*

*and those who make light of their labours.*
*When the unrighteous see them,*
*    they will be shaken with dreadful fear,*
*    and they will be amazed at the unexpected salvation*
*        of the righteous . . .*

*But the righteous live forever,*
*    and their reward is with the Lord;*
*the Most High takes care of them.*
*Therefore they will receive a glorious crown*
*    and a beautiful diadem from the hand of the Lord,*
*because with his right hand he will cover them*
*    and with his arm he will shield them.*[163]

These passages, it seems to me, demonstrate beyond reasonable doubt that the 'immortality' spoken of in the first passage is the same as the temporary rest in 'heaven' of which Josephus spoke as preceding the resurrection itself. There is a clear time-sequence: first, the righteous die, and the unrighteous celebrate; then, a further event at which the unrighteous will discover their mistake when confronted with the righteous as their judges. No doubt some Hellenistic readers of the Wisdom of Solomon might have missed the point in a casual reading. But against the full Jewish background the book seems to represent the majority position rather than a Hellenization.[164]

If we want to find the latter, we turn, not surprisingly, to Philo:

*When Abraham left this mortal life, 'he is added to the*
*people of God' [quoting Genesis 25.8], in that he inherited*
*incorruption and became equal to the angels.*[165]

*[Moses] represents the good man as not dying but*
*departing . . . He would have the nature of the fully purified*
*soul shewn as unquenchable and immortal, destined to*

*journey from hence to heaven, not to meet with dissolution*
*and corruption, which death appears to bring.*[166]

When people die, much of the personality is laid in the grave with
them;

*but if anywhere . . . there grows up a virtue-loving tendency,*
*it is saved from extinction by memories, which are a means of*
*keeping alive the flame of noble qualities.*[167]

This perspective was not confined to Hellenistic, or Alexandrian,
speculative philosophers. It also emerges, for instance, in an apocalyptic work: in the Testament of Abraham, the angels are instructed to
take Abraham into Paradise,

*where there are the tents of my righteous ones and [where] the*
*mansions of my holy ones, Isaac and Jacob, are in his bosom,*
*where there is no toil, no grief, no moaning, but peace and*
*exultation and endless life.*[168]

There appear, then, to be three basic positions taken by Jews in
our period, with, no doubt, minor modifications within each. The
Sadducees stand out as unusual in that they will have nothing to do
with a future life, neither with immortality nor with resurrection. No
doubt a substantial and perhaps growing minority of Jews, including
those who have quite clearly drunk deeply from the Platonic and general Hellenistic well, could write of the immortality of the soul. But the
majority speak of the bodily resurrection of the dead; and frequently
address the problem of an intermediate state; this last point is itself
strong evidence for belief in bodily resurrection, since only on this
premise is there a problem to be addressed. Sometimes, in describing
this latter state, they borrow Hellenistic language which in its own

context denotes a *permanent* disembodied state; but they still make it clear that bodily resurrection is the end they have in sight.

Why did the belief in resurrection arise, and how did it fit in with the broader Jewish worldview and belief-system which I have sketched in my *New Testament and the People of God*? Again and again we have seen that this belief is bound up with the struggle to maintain obedience to Israel's ancestral laws in the face of persecution. Resurrection is the divine reward for martyrs; it is what will happen after the great tribulation. But it is not simply a special reward for those who have undergone special sufferings. Rather, the eschatological expectation of most Jews of this period was for a renewal, not an abandonment, of the present space-time order as a whole, and themselves within it. Since this was based on the justice and mercy of the creator god, the god of Israel, it was inconceivable that those who had died in the struggle to bring the new world into being should be left out of the blessing when it eventually broke upon the nation and thence on the world.[169]

The old metaphor of corpses coming to life had, ever since Ezekiel at least, been one of the most vivid ways of *de*noting the return from exile and *con*noting the renewal of the covenant and of all creation. Within the context of persecution and struggle for Torah in the Syrian and Roman periods, this metaphor itself acquired a new life. If Israel's god would 'raise' his people (metaphorically) by bringing them back from their continuing exile, he would also, within that context, 'raise' those people (literally) who had died in the hope of that national and covenantal vindication. 'Resurrection', while focusing attention on the new embodiment of the individuals involved, retained its original sense of the restoration of Israel by her covenant god. As such, 'resurrection' was not simply a pious hope about new life for dead people. It carried with it all that was associated with the return from exile itself: forgiveness of sins, the re-establishment of Israel as the true humanity of the covenant god, and the renewal of all creation.[170] Indeed, resurrection and the renewal of creation go hand in hand. If the space-time world were to disappear, resurrection would not make sense. Alternatively, if there was to be no resurrection, who would people the renewed cosmos?

Thus the Jews who believed in resurrection did so as one part of a larger belief in the renewal of the whole created order. Resurrection would be, in one and the same moment, the reaffirmation of the covenant and the reaffirmation of creation. Israel would be restored within a restored cosmos: the world would see, at last, who had all along been the true people of the creator god.[171] This is where the twin Jewish 'basic beliefs' finally come together. Monotheism and election, taken together, demand eschatology. Creational/covenantal monotheism, taken together with the tension between election and exile, demands resurrection and a new world. That is why some of the prophets used gorgeous mythical language to describe what would happen: lions and lambs lying down together, trees bearing fruit every month, Jerusalem becoming like a new Eden. This, too, was simply the outworking, in poetic symbol, of the basic belief that the creator of the universe was Israel's god, and vice versa. When he acted, there would be a great celebration. All creation, in principle, would join in.

To write this seems almost uncontroversial as a historical summary of Jewish belief. Dozens of texts of the period point this way; we are on absolutely firm historical ground. Sanders, summarizing the Jewish hope in this period, writes:

> *Many Jews looked forward to a new and better age . . .*
> *The hopes centred on the restoration of the people, the*
> *building or purification of the temple and Jerusalem, the*
> *defeat or conversion of the Gentiles, and the establishment*
> *of purity and righteousness . . . The hope that God would*
> *fundamentally change things was a perfectly reasonable hope*
> *for people to hold who read the Bible and who believed that*
> *God had created the world and had sometimes intervened*
> *dramatically to save his people.*[172]

What Sanders never does, however, is to draw out the highly polemical nature of this claim in the context of the twentieth-century reading of first-century Jewish texts, including the texts of those first-century Jews who called themselves Christians.[173] But the point must surely be drawn out. Within the mainline Jewish writings of this period, covering a wide range of styles, genres, political persuasions and theological perspectives, *there is virtually no evidence that Jews were expecting the end of the space-time universe.* There is abundant evidence that they, like Jeremiah and others before them, knew a good metaphor when they saw one, and used cosmic imagery to bring out the full theological significance of cataclysmic socio-political events. There is almost nothing to suggest that they followed the Stoics into the belief that the world itself would come to an end; and there is almost everything—their stories, their symbols, their praxis, not least their tendency to revolution, and their entire theology—to suggest that they did not.

What, then, did they believe was going to happen? They believed that *the present world order* would come to an end—the world order in which pagans held power, and Jews, the covenant people of the creator god, did not.[174] Sects like the Essenes believed that the present order, in which the wrong Jews held power, would come to an end, and a new world order would be inaugurated in which the right Jews, i.e. themselves, attained power instead. We cannot, of course, rule out the possibility that some Jews believed that the physical world would come to an end, just as we cannot rule out the possibility that some Jews thought there were five gods, or that the Egyptians were the one chosen people of the creator god. But such views are marginal not only to the literature of all sorts that we possess from the period, but to the worldview of the great majority of (non-writing) first-century Jews, which we can reconstruct from their symbols, their stories and above all their praxis. Jews simply did not believe that the space-time order was shortly to disappear.

At a seminar at the Society of Biblical Literature Annual Meeting in November 1989, I listened to Professor John Collins expound a

view of Jewish eschatology not dissimilar to that which I have just outlined. At the end I suggested that if Albert Schweitzer had heard that
paper a hundred years ago, the entire course of New Testament studies
in the twentieth century would have been different. Collins, with due
modesty, agreed that that might well be the case.[175] Schweitzer was
right, I believe, when at the beginning of the twentieth century he
drew attention to apocalyptic as the matrix of early Christianity. It is
now high time, as the century draws towards its close, to state, against
Schweitzer, what that apocalyptic matrix actually was and meant.

It should be noted most emphatically that, although 'resurrection' is naturally something that individuals can hope for, for themselves or for those they love, the belief we have studied is always
focused on a *general* resurrection at the end of the present age and the
start of the age to come. This will be a raising to life in which all Israel
(with suitable exceptions, depending on one's point of view) will share.
Seen from one angle, it will constitute Israel's *salvation*: after the long
years of oppression and desolation, she will be rescued at last. From
another angle, it will constitute Israel's *vindication* (or 'justification'):
having claimed throughout her history to be the people of the creator
god, the resurrection will at last make the claim good. Creational and
covenantal monotheism, and the eschatology to which they give birth,
thus form a context within which what is sometimes called 'Jewish
soteriology', the beliefs that Jews held about salvation, may be situated
accurately and fruitfully. It is important that we spell this out a little
further.

## 6. Salvation and Justification

The word 'salvation' would denote, to a first-century Jew, the hope
which we have studied throughout this chapter, seen particularly in
terms of Israel's rescue, by her god, from pagan oppression. This would
be the gift of Israel's god to his whole people, all at once. Individual
Jews would find their own 'salvation' through their membership within

Israel, that is, within the covenant: covenant membership in the present was the guarantee (more or less) of 'salvation' in the future.

We have already seen how first-century Jews understood covenant membership. The whole Jewish worldview, with its stories, its symbols, and its praxis, gives a clear answer. The covenant was entered through Jewish birth or proselyte initiation; it was sealed, for males, in the fact of circumcision; it was maintained through fidelity to the covenant document, Torah. This is most significant: as Sanders has argued extensively, membership in the covenant is *demonstrated*, rather than *earned*, by possession of Torah and the attempt to keep it. When the age to come dawns, those who have remained faithful to the covenant will be vindicated; this does not mean 'those who have kept Torah completely', since the sacrificial system existed precisely to enable Israelites who knew themselves to be sinful to maintain their membership none the less. And the attempt to keep Torah, whether more or less successful, was normally and regularly understood as response, not as human initiative. This is Sanders' thesis, and, despite some criticisms that have been launched, it seems to me thus far completely correct as a description of first-century Judaism.[176]

It is within this context that there arose, within our period, debates as to who precisely would be vindicated when the covenant god finally acted to liberate Israel. 'All Israel has a share in the age to come'; but not Sadducees, not those who deny Torah, not Epicureans.[177] The sectaries who wrote the Scrolls would have agreed with the sentiment, but with a different list of exclusions: they and they alone were 'Israel', and the Pharisees ('the speakers of smooth things') and the official Temple hierarchy were definitely to share the lot of the Sons of Darkness. We can be fairly sure that the different factions in the war threw similar anathemas at one another.

The first-century question of soteriology then becomes: what are the badges of membership that mark one out in the group that is to be saved, vindicated, raised to life (in the case of members already dead) or exalted to power (in the case of those still alive)? For the

Pharisees, there was a programme of intensification of Torah. For the Essenes, there was a (varying) set of communal rules, and an appeal to loyalty to a Teacher. For many rebel groups, there were subtly differing agendas, probably including, in the case of the Sicarii, loyalty to a would-be dynasty, and, in the case of the Zealots in the narrow sense, loyalty to a particular agenda and, at one stage at least, to a particular leader (Simon bar Giora). For Josephus, it was quite different: rescue, in the very practical sense, came by acknowledging that Israel's god had gone over to the Romans, and by following suit.

In all of these cases we are witnessing different interpretations of the fundamental Jewish soteriology. The sequence of thought is precisely that of the many stories we examined earlier as representative of the basic Jewish worldview, and may be set out logically as follows:

a. The creator god calls Israel to be his people;
b. Israel, currently in 'exile', is to be redeemed, precisely because she is the covenant people of this god;
c. Present loyalty to the covenant is the sign of future redemption;
d. Loyalty to this covenant is being tested at this moment of crisis;
e. At this moment, what counts as loyalty, and hence what marks out those who will be saved/vindicated/raised to life, is . . . [with the different groups filling in the blank according to their own agendas].

We have already seen that a great deal of Jewish literature of the period tells this story in some shape or form.

What matters, then, is not simply (in Sanders' categories) 'getting in' (how one becomes a member of the covenant) and 'staying in' (how one remains a member of the covenant). What matters, when Israel's symbols are under threat—when the question of what it means to be a Jew is everywhere raised and nowhere settled—is staying in *at this time of crisis*; or, to put it another way, staying in when there was a risk of finding oneself suddenly outside, or, perhaps, getting back in after finding oneself suddenly excluded.[178] That is the situation that sects exploit. It is exactly the situation that we find in first-century Palestine.

What counts above all at a time like that is adherence to the right symbols: not simply the mainline symbols of Temple, Torah and Land, because the rival groups claim them as well, but the symbols which show that one is a member of the correct sub-group. Those who die a martyr's death rather than break Torah will receive their bodies again (said the Maccabaean martyrs).[179] Those who 'have faith in' the Teacher of Righteousness will be delivered (said some of the Essenes).[180] Those who pull down the eagle from the Temple gate can look forward to a glorious resurrection (said the teachers who were egging them on).[181] Those who follow Menahem will be vindicated when the war is won (said his Sicarii followers).[182] Those who follow our strict interpretation of Torah, according to the tradition of the fathers, will be vindicated as true Israelites (said the rabbis, and some of their putative Pharisaic predecessors).[183] This is soteriology in practice, first-century style. It has little or nothing to do with moralizing or the quiet practice of abstract virtue. It has to do with life after death only to the extent that, if one dies before the great day dawns (especially if one dies as a martyr in the struggle), one needs to be assured that one will not be left out when salvation arrives, complete with restored Temple, cleansed Land, and Israel exalted at last over her enemies.

This is the point when a vital theological move can be made. When the age to come finally arrives, those who are the true covenant members will be vindicated; but, if one already knows the signs and symbols which mark out those true covenant members, this vindication, this 'justification', *can be seen already in the present time.* Covenant faithfulness in the present is the sign of covenantal vindication in the future; the badges of that present covenant faithfulness may vary from group to group, but those who wear the appropriate ones are assured that the true god will remain faithful to them and bring them safely into the new world that will soon be ushered in. We may again take the

Essenes as an example. To suffer with the elect, to cling to the Teacher of Righteousness, and to abide by his teaching—this would be the sign *in the present* that one belonged to the group which, though marginal for the moment, would be vindicated as the true Israel in the future. The covenant god had renewed his covenant with this group, and they could therefore trust his covenant faithfulness (*tsedaqah*, 'righteousness'), that he would vindicate them, giving them favourable judgment (*mishpat*, 'justification') as his new-covenant people, when his action, at present secret, at last became public:

> *As for me,*
> *my justification is with God.*
> *In His hand are the perfection of my way*
> *and the uprightness of my heart.*
> *He will wipe out my transgression*
> *through his righteousness.*
>
> *From the source of His righteousness*
> *is my justification*
> *and from His marvellous mysteries*
> *is the light in my heart.*
>
> *As for me,*
> *if I stumble, the mercies of God*
> *shall be my eternal salvation.*
>
> *If I stagger because of the sin of flesh,*
> *my justification shall be*
> *by the righteousness of God which endures for ever.*[184]

Justification is *both* future (the vindication, the 'judgment', when Israel's god finally acts) *and* present. Both depend on the divine covenant faithfulness; both will occur despite the continuing sinfulness of the worshipper. The present justification is secret, and depends simply on maintaining valid membership in the sect. The justification to come will be public, and will consist of the victory of the sect, and the establishment of its members as the true rulers of Israel and hence of the world.

How then does one become a member of the group that will inherit this glorious destiny, and who may perhaps believe that the future vindication can be anticipated, albeit secretly, in the present? Clearly, in the case of a sect, it is a matter of choice. To the extent that the Essenes were celibate, one could not join by birth. But the Scrolls teach quite clearly that this choice reflects an antecedent divine choice. This is simply the natural extension of regular biblical teaching. Deuteronomy made it quite clear that Israel was the people of the creator god, not because Israel was special, but because this god simply loved her.[185] The Essenes were, they believed, the true Israel; therefore, what was true of Israel was true of them. They were the elect ones, chosen to bear the destiny of Israel into the age to come.[186] There is no reason to suppose that any Jewish group or sect would have thought any differently.

Salvation, then, was a matter of a new world, the renewal of creation. Within this, Israel's god would call some from within the nation to be a new Israel, the spearhead of the divine purpose. Within this again, this renewed people were to be the holy, pure, renewed human beings, living in a covenant fidelity which would answer to the covenant faithfulness of the creator god, and which would end in the renewal, i.e. resurrection, of human bodies themselves. When this god acted, those who belonged, by his grace alone, to this group, would be rescued, and thereby vindicated as the true people of god that they had claimed to be all along. Those who had died in advance of that day would be raised in order to share it. It is thus, within the context of the entire future hope of Israel, and in particular within the context of the promise of resurrection, that we can understand the essentially simple lines of second-temple Jewish soteriology. The doctrines of justification and salvation belong within the story we have seen all along to characterize the fundamental Jewish worldview.

## 7. Conclusion: First-Century Judaism

I have argued in this essay for a particular way of understanding the hope which, in its varied forms, was embraced by Jews in the two centuries on either side of the turn of the eras. This completes our survey, in this essay (and Part III of my *New Testament and the People of God*), of the second-temple Jewish history, worldview and belief-system. For the most part this has not been intentionally controversial, though no doubt some will want to challenge this or that aspect of my case. Any resulting controversy, actually, is quite likely to arise not in relation to Judaism in itself but from the effect of this reconstruction upon readings of early Christianity.

I have tried to show above all that, despite the wide variety of emphasis, praxis and literature for which we have ample evidence, which indeed justify us in speaking of 'Judaisms' in relation to this period, we can trace the outlines of a worldview, and a belief-system, which can properly be thought of as 'mainline', and which were shared by a large number of Jews at the time. Having begun with the history, we moved on to the stories which were told by the Jews who lived out that history, the symbols which were common to those who told those stories, and the praxis that went with those symbols. From this, and from the literature we possess, we have now examined the basic belief-system of first-century Jews, and have looked in particular at the hope which they cherished, a hope which drew together symbol, story and belief and turned it into worship, prayer and action. The explanatory circle is complete. It was within this history that we discovered this hope; it was because of this hope that this history turned out as it did.

It was to a people cherishing this hope, and living in this (often muddled) state of tension and aspiration, that there came a prophet in the Jordan wilderness, calling the people to repent and to undergo a baptism for 'the forgiveness of sins', and warning them that Israel was about to pass through a fiery judgment out of which a new people of Abraham would be forged. It was to this same people that another prophet came, announcing in the villages of Galilee that now at last Israel's god was becoming king. We should not be surprised at what happened next.

## Abbreviations

**cf.** confer
**Compendia** *Compendia Rerum Iudaicarum ad Novum Testamentum.* Section One: *The Jewish People in the First Century,* ed. S. Safrai and M. Stern. 2 vols. Section Two: *The Literature of the Jewish People in the Period of the Second Temple and the Talmud,* ed. M. J. Mulder, M. E. Stone and S. Safrai. 3 vols. Philadelphia: Fortress; Assen/Maastricht: Van Gorcum. 1976–87.
**cp.** compare
**esp.** especially
**Jos.** Josephus
**LXX** Septuagint version of the Old Testament (see later in this discussion)
**PG** J. P. Migne, *Patrologia Graeca.* Paris, 1857–66.
**SB** H. L. Strack and P. Billerbeck, *Kommentar zum Neuen Testament aus Talmud und Midrasch.* 6 vols. Munich: C. H. Beck, 1926–56.
**Schürer** E. Schürer, *The History of the Jewish People in the Age of Jesus Christ (175 B.C.–A.D. 135).* Rev. & ed. M. Black, G. Vermes, F. G. B. Millar. 4 vols. Edinburgh: T & T Clark, 1973–87.
**Suet.** Suetonius
**Tac.** Tacitus
**TDNT** *Theological Dictionary of the New Testament,* ed. G. Kittel and G. Friedrich. 10 vols. Trans. & ed. G. W. Bromiley. Grand Rapids, Mich.: Eerdmans, 1964–76.

## Notes

1 I here follow (more or less) Collins 1979, 1987. The latter, together with Rowland 1982, forms a good recent introduction to the whole subject.

2 See Hellholm 1983; Aune 1987, ch. 7.

3 cf. the full definition given by Collins 1987, 4: 'a genre of revelatory literature with a narrative framework, in which a revelation is mediated by an other-worldly being to a human recipient, disclosing a transcendent reality which is both temporal, in so far as it envisages eschatological salvation, and spatial in so far as it involves another, supernatural world'.

4 *Apoc. Abr.* 12.3–10.

5 *2 Bar.* 36.1–37.1.

6 cf. ch. 3 in my *New Testament and the People of God.*

7 Fountain: Zech. 13.1; cf. Jer. 2.13. Vine, cedar: Ps. 80.8–19; Isa. 5.1–7; Ezek. 17.1–24.

8 See Part II, chs. 3, 5 in my *New Testament and the People of God.* I here follow Caird 1980, ch. 14.

9 e.g. Isa. 51.9–11.

10 *T. Mos.* 10.5: see later in this discussion. Jeremiah used 'cosmic' language about the unmaking of creation to refer to the events of the exile: Jer. 4.23–8 (see later in this discussion).

11 cf. *Apoc. Abr.* 19, 20, describing similar visions (as do many such texts) to the chariot-vision in Ezek. 1. On this whole theme see Gruenwald 1980.

12 See now particularly Stone 1990.

13 James Callaghan, on taking office in March 1976.

14 See Caird 1980, ch. 14; Rowland 1982; Koch 1972; Hellholm 1983; Collins 1987; Stone 1984; etc.

15 See Schweitzer 1954 [1910], 1968b [1931].

16 Caird, loc. cit.; see Glasson 1977; Borg 1987. Cf. too Cranfield 1982.

17 I am grateful to Prof. R. D. Williams for pointing this out to me.

18 On all this, see vol. 3 in the Christian Origins and the Question of God series.

19 'Apokalyptic ist bei mir stets als Naherwartung verstanden' ('for me, apocalyptic always means imminent-expectation'), in a letter from Ernst Käsemann to the present author, dated 18 January 1983. See Käsemann 1969, chs. 4–5.

20 On the idea of resurrection, and its place within this structure of thought, see section 5 later in this discussion. A good example

of a firmly this-worldly eschatology, though still invested with glorious overtones, can be found in *Sib. Or.* 3.500–800.

21  John Bunyan, *Pilgrim's Progress*. The first quotation is the opening sentence of the book, the second is taken from 'The author's apology for his book' which forms a preface.

22  Amos 7.7–9; Jer. 1.13; Ezek. 17.1–24. The question of whether some of these are 'natural', and some 'supernatural', visions is beside the point here.

23  This is particularly clear in the case of *T. 12 Patr.*: see Nickelsburg 1981, 231–41; Schürer 3.767–81; Collins 1984, 342f.

24  Jos. *Ant.* 10.208, interpreting Dan. 2.36–8. In 4QpNah. 1.6–9 the 'lion' clearly stands for an individual, normally taken to be Alexander Jannaeus.

25  2 Sam. 12.1–15.

26  1 Sam. 17.

27  '. . . So YHWH opened the eyes of the servant, and he saw; the mountain was full of horses and chariots of fire all around Elisha.'

28  e.g. Ps. 84.9.

29  It is impossible to enter into detailed debate about this complex passage. For recent discussions, with extensive bibliography, see Goldingay 1989, 137–93; Casey 1991.

30  So Hooker 1967, 71ff.

31  See section 4 later in this discussion; and vol. 2 in the Christian Origins and the Question of God series.

32  The point at which Josephus omits to mention Dan. 7 (*Ant.* 10.267f.) in his otherwise near-complete account of the book is also the point at which (cf. Moule 1977, 14, 16) he stresses how highly his Jewish contemporaries regarded Daniel as a prophet for their time. The reuse of ideas from Dan. 7 in e.g. *1 En.* 37–71; *4 Ezra* 11–13; *2 Bar.* 39 (on all of which, see later in this discussion), shows that he was correct in this. This point, amplified in much of the argument to come, tells heavily against the insistence of Casey 1991 on subjecting all question of a reference to Dan. 7 to primarily *linguistic* tests; what counts even more than linguistic usage is the way the entire chapter, which forms the vital context of the crucial v. 13, was read and understood at the time.

33  See Goldingay 1989, 157f.: ch. 7 rounds off a chiasm that began with ch. 2. Professor Moule suggests to me in a letter a cautionary

note: it is possible that 'the Aramaic bits in both books [i.e. Daniel and Ezra] are fortuitous, and probably due to the copyist's having a defective exemplar, and, faute de mieux, filling in the lacunae from an Aramaic Targum'.

34 See ch. 8 in my *New Testament and the People of God.*

35 Nor is there any necessary idea here of this vindication including the end of the space-time order. The doctrine of resurrection, developing as it was at the same time and under the same pressures, indicates that the present world would continue, with the righteous people of the covenant god now in control under his sole sovereignty, and the righteous dead returning to share in the triumph. See later in this discussion.

36 See Cohen 1987, 197.

37 See the detailed account of research in Goldingay 1989, 169–72.

38 Collins 1987, 81–3. Cf. Goldingay 1989, 171f.

39 cf. ch. 9 in my *New Testament and the People of God,* pp. 262–8.

40 Following e.g. Moule 1977, 13. That this reference at least must include human beings is acknowledged by Collins 1987, 83.

41 cf. ch. 9 above, pp. 268–72.

42 Jer. 4.23–8, speaking of the coming destruction of Judah and her Temple, and investing that space-time reality with a theological interpretation: this is like the unmaking of creation itself.

43 This has then been transferred to some readings of early Christian literature: see Mack 1988 for a sustained polemic against the supposed radical dualism of Mark's gospel.

44 On the different ways in which this hope might be expressed by different groups of Jews, see later in this discussion, and also ch. 7 in my *New Testament and the People of God.* On the Jewish hope see now Sanders 1992, ch. 14, and his summaries on e.g. 298.

45 *ha-'olam hazeh* and *ha-'olam haba'.* On the two ages see e.g. Schürer 2.495.

46 e.g. in Schürer 2, 488–554, where 'Messianism' really means 'the future hope' (which sometimes contains messianic expectation).

47 Isa. 2.2–4; Mic. 4.1–3; Zech. 8.20–3.

48 Ps. 2.8–9; *Ps. Sol.* 17–18.

49 cf. 1 Macc. 14.12, with its echoes of 1 Kgs. 4.25; Mic. 4.4, etc. On 'salvation' in Judaism cf. esp. Loewe 1981. At this point many recent interpreters have not, I think, gone far enough in

rethinking the Jewish material; even Sanders continues to refer to 'salvation' as though it were an easy and univocal term (e.g. 1992, 350, 441).

50 See Sanders 1992, 278: 'national survival looms much larger than does individual life after death'; cf. also 298.

51 Zeph. 3.14–20.

52 See ch. 9 in my *New Testament and the People of God*.

53 Isa. 54.4–8; cf. Hos., *passim*.

54 Jer. 31.31ff.; Ezek. 11.19f.; 36.22–32; cf. 39.29; Joel 2.28, and also Isa. 32.15; Zech. 12.10. In the Scrolls, cf. 1QS 1.16–2.25; 1QH 5.11f.; 7.6f.; 9.32; 12.12; 14.13; 16.7, 12; 17.26; 1Q34bis 2.5–7; 4QDibHam 5. Cf. Cross 1958, 164 n.40.

55 Dt. 10.16; 29.6; 30.6; Jer. 4.4; 31.33; 32.39, 40; Ezek. 11.19; 36.26–7; 44.7. The charge of 'spiritual uncircumcision' makes the same point negatively: cf. Lev. 26.41; Jer. 9.23ff.; Ezek. 44.7; Ex. 6.12, 30 (lips); Jer. 6.10 (ear). This theme, too, reappears in the Scrolls: 1QS 5.5; 1QpHab 11.13 (for the negative side see Leaney 1966, 167) and in early Christian literature (Ac. 7.51; Rom. 2.2.6–9; *Barn.* 9, *passim*; 10.12). See SB 3.126; *TDNT* 6.76ff. (R. Meyer).

56 Jos. *Ant.* 18.23, pointing out that the only difference between the 'Zealots' and the Pharisees is the degree of passion with which their desire for liberty is held. That the view was held over a long period of time is affirmed in *War* 7.323. See the discussions in Goodman 1987, 93f. Hengel 1989 (1961), 71–3, 86f., and esp. 90–110; Sanders 1992, 282f.

57 Jos. *Ant.* 18.3–5; submitting to the census, they argued, 'carried with it a status amounting to downright slavery'.

58 *Ant.* 17.149–63.

59 *Ant.* 18.24; *War* 7.323ff.

60 See Sanders 1992, 282; and see again *Ant.* 18.23: 'they think little of submitting to death . . . if only they may avoid calling any man master'. Cf. *War* 2.433, 443: Menahem, said by Josephus to be the descendant of Judas the Galilean, and to share his doctrine of 'no King but God', is himself killed by a group that takes this so literally as not to want Menahem himself as a ruler.

61 See Jos. *War* 4.151–61 on the Zealot's appointment of a new high priest; *Ant.* 13.288–92 on Pharisaic opposition to Hyrcanus'

holding of the high priesthood. On the attitude of the Essenes see e.g. Schürer 2.582 (for texts see e.g. 1QM 2, which lays plans for the installation of a true high priesthood while the holy war is in progress). See now Rofé 1988 for suggestions that this polemic considerably antedates the second century.

62  See Part IV in my *New Testament and the People of God*.

63  Goodman 1987, 108.

64  As Goodman 1987 argues in the case of the puppet Jewish aristocracy.

65  There is clear evidence of the religious devotion of the revolutionaries on e.g. Masada: see chs. 6–7 in my *New Testament and the People of God*.

66  Ps. 145.10–13; cf. Pss. 93, 96, 97, etc.

67  Isa. 33.22.

68  Isa. 52.7. The whole passage is instructive, seeing the end of exile, the return of YHWH to Zion, as the answer to the oppression of Israel and the inauguration of the universal reign of Israel's god. The selling of this passage immediately before the fourth servant song (52.13–53.12) provides further food for thought. Cf. Zeph. 3.14–20, with the kingship motif in v. 15.

69  See chs. 7–8 in my *New Testament and the People of God*.

70  Loeb edn., 6.275; cf. Sanders 1992, 289, who says, in dramatic if imprecise confirmation of our present point, that 'even the present-day reader of Daniel can see that the stone that breaks all other kingdoms is *the Kingdom of God, Israel*' (my italics).

71  For Josephus' view of Daniel as a prophet of great significance see the previous discussion, p. 266, and esp. *Ant.* 10.266–8; for his application of Dan. 8.21 to Alexander the Great, *Ant.* 11.337; of 11.31 and 7.25 to the Maccabaean period, 12.322; of Dan. 11–12 to the rise of Rome and the fall of Jerusalem, 10.276–7. Instead of exploring these last any further, Josephus turns aside instead to a general comment about the folly of the Epicureans in denying the doctrine of providence.

72  Tac. *Hist.* 5.13; Suet. *Vesp.* 4. Josephus claims that he himself prophesied to Vespasian that he would become emperor: *War* 3.399–408. See further later in this discussion (or pp. 312f. in my *New Testament and the People of God*).

145 *War* 7.349f. Cf. Lane Fox 1986, 149–67, including a passage from the fourth-century philosopher and alchemist Synesius (PG 66.1317, quoted by Lane Fox, 149f.) which is very close to Eleazar's speech at this point. Clearly the idea was widespread in both time and space.

146 *War* 1.650, repeated substantially by the culprits themselves in 1.653.

147 *Ant.* 17.152f.

148 Ps. Sol. 3.11f. (14f.) (tr. S. P. Brock in Sparks 1984, 659). On resurrection in *Ps. Sol.* see Nickelsburg 1972, 131–4.

149 R. B. Wright, in Charlesworth 1985, 655. See also Sanders 1977, 388.

150 Mt. 22.23, 34 and pars.; Ac. 23.6–9, cf. 4.1f.; mAb. 4.22; mSanh. 10.1 (on which see Urbach 1987 [1975, 1979], 652, and the notes [991f.] on mBer. 5.2; mSot. 9.15). The second of the Eighteen Benedictions praises the creator for making the dead alive.

151 Ac. 4.1f.

152 Jn. 12.10f.

153 See e.g. Lk. 9.7, 19.

154 Sanders 1985, 237; more cautiously, 1992, 303.

155 These two groups would, of course, be likely to overlap quite heavily; i.e. political and philosophical assimilation would go together, both causing the assimilators to tone down the mainline Jewish expectation.

156 Sometimes misleadingly called the *Apocalypse of Moses*: see Schürer 3.757.

157 *Adam and Eve* 41.3; 43.2f.; 51.2.

158 *1 En.* 51.1–5; cf. 90.33; 91.10. On the personal eschatology of *1 En.* see Schürer 2.541f.

159 4 Ezra 7.32; cf. 7.97; *2 Bar.* 30.1; 50.1–4. 4 Ezra also speaks of the period of waiting between death and resurrection, which is clear evidence of a hope other than simply the immortality of the soul: 4.35; 7.95, 101; cf. *2 Bar.* 30.2.

160 *T. Jud.* 25.1–5 (the quote is from 4–5). Cf. *T. Benj.* 10.2–9.

161 See Nickelsburg 1972, *passim*.

162 Wisd. 3.1–4; cf. 4.7; 5.15f.; 6.17–20. In the last passage there is a sequence: desire for instruction leads to love of wisdom, thence

to keeping of her laws, and thence to 'assurance of immortality', which in turn 'brings one near to God': 'so the desire for wisdom leads to a kingdom'. Cf. too Tob. 3.6, 10.

163 Wisd. 3.6–8; 4.16f.; 4.20–5.2; 5.15f.

164 Wisd. 5.1 used the verb *stesetai*, cognate with *anastasis*, 'resurrection'; cf. too the LXX of 2 Sam. 7.12. *kai anasteso to sperma sou meta se*, 'and I will raise up your seed after you . . .'

165 Philo, *Sac.* 5. Is there an echo of this belief in Lk. 20.36?

166 Philo, *Heir* 276.

167 Philo, *Migr.* 16.

168 *T. Abr.* [recension A] 20.14 (tr. E. P. Sanders in Charlesworth 1983, 895). Sanders points out, in his note ad loc., the illogicality of Isaac and Jacob preceding Abraham into Paradise, and of Abraham's bosom somehow being there in advance as well. On Paradise as originally a temporary staging-post in a longer journey, which gradually became identified in later Jewish works with the goal of the journey itself, see Schürer 2.541f.

169 This goes back, *mutatis mutandis*, at least as far as Ps. 49.15; 73.24.

170 Sanders 1992, 303, sets the Jewish belief in an afterlife side by side with the belief in a new world order, but makes no attempt to trace the connection between them. C. H. Cave, in Schürer 2.546f., provides a classic example of holding apart things that should be kept together.

171 We may compare again the graphic scene in Wisd. 3–5.

172 Sanders 1992, 298, 303; cf. 456f.

173 The closest he comes, I think, is at 1992, 368, where he says that the dramatic change in the future, to which the Qumran sect looked forward, should not be called 'the eschaton', 'the last [event]', as modern scholars often do call it, 'since like other Jews the Essenes did not think that the world would end'.

174 Sanders 1985 uses phrases like 'the present world order' in a somewhat different sense, keeping the option open of a less spatio-temporal future hope. He seems now (1992) to have come down more firmly on the line that I have taken.

175 It is only fair to say that I think Collins would still disagree with several of the details of this essay (and Part III of my *New Testament and the People of God*).

176  See Sanders 1977, 1983, and now 1992, 262–78. I shall discuss the criticisms elsewhere.

177  mSanh. 10.1. The fact that Akiba is then quoted as making an addition to the list (to include a ban on those who read the heretical books, or who attempt magical cures) indicates that the basic saying is earlier, at the latest in the second half of the first century AD.

178  cf. Harper 1988.

179  2 Macc. 7, etc.

180  1QpHab 8.1–3, interpreting a text (Hab. 2.4) well known to readers of the NT (Rom. 1.17; Gal. 3.11).

181  *War* 1.648–50.

182  cf. *War* 2.433–48.

183  mSanh. 10.1.

184  1QS 11.2–3, 5, 11–12.

185  Dt. 7.7f., etc.

186  On election in the Scrolls see e.g. Vermes 1987 [1962], 41–6.

## Bibliography

Beasley-Murray, G. R. 1986. *Jesus and the Kingdom of God*. Grand Rapids, Mich.: Eerdmans.

Beckwith, Roger T. 1981. 'Daniel 9 and the Date of Messiah's Coming in Essene, Hellenistic, Pharisaic, Zealot and Early Christian Computation.' *Révue de Qumran* 40:521–42.

Borg, Marcus J. 1987. 'An Orthodoxy Reconsidered: The "End-of-the-World Jesus"' In *The Glory of Christ in the New Testament: Studies in Christology in Memory of George Bradford Caird*, ed. L. D. Hurst and N. T. Wright, 207–17. Oxford: OUP.

Caird, George B. 1980. *The Language and Imagery of the Bible*. London: Duckworth.

Casey, P. Maurice. 1991. 'Method in Our Madness, and Madness in Their Methods. Some Approaches to the Son of Man Problem in Recent Scholarship.' *Journal for the Study of the New Testament* 42:17–43.

Charlesworth, James H., ed. 1983. *The Old Testament Pseudepigrapha*. Vol. 1. *Apocalyptic Literature and Testaments*. Garden City, N.Y.: Doubleday.

————, ed. 1985. *The Old Testament Pseudepigrapha*. Vol. 2. *Expansions of the 'Old Testament' and Legends, Wisdom and Philosophical Literature, Prayers, Psalms and Odes, Fragments of Lost Judaeo-Hellenistic Works*. Garden City, N.Y.: Doubleday.

Cohen, Shaye J.D. 1987. *From the Maccabees to the Mishnah*. In *Library of Early Christianity*, ed. Wayne A. Meeks. Philadelphia: Westminster Press.

Collins, John J., ed. 1979. *Apocalypse: The Morphology of a Genre*. Semeia, vol. 14. Missoula, Mont.: Scholars Press.

————. 1984. 'Testaments.' In *Compendia* 2.2325–55.

————. 1987. *The Apocalyptic Imagination*. New York: Crossroad. Stephen W. Sykes, 22–34. Cambridge: CUP.

Cranfield, Charles E. B. 1982. 'Thoughts on New Testament Eschatology.' *Scottish Journal of Theology* 35:497–512.

Glasson, T. F. 1977. 'Schweitzer's Influence—Blessing or Bane?' *Journal of Theological Studies* 28:289–302.

Goldingay, John E. 1989. *Daniel*. Word Biblical Commentary, vol. 30. Dallas, Tex.: Word Books.

Goodman, Martin. 1987. *The Rating Class of Judaea: The Origins of the Jewish Revolt Against Rome A.D. 66–70*. Cambridge: CUP.

Gruenwald, Ithamar. 1980. *Apocalyptic and Merkavah Mysticism*. Arbeiten zur Geschichte des Antiken Judentums und des Urchristentums, vol. 14. Leiden: Brill.

Harper, George. 1988. *Repentance in Pauline Theology*. Ph.D. Dissertation, McGill University, Montreal.

Harvey, Anthony E. 1982. *Jesus and the Constraints of History: The Bampton Lectures, 1980*. London: Duckworth.

Hellholm, David. 1983. *Apocalypticism in the Mediterranean World and the Near East: Proceeding of the International Colloquium on Apocalypticism, Uppsala, August 12–17, 1979*. Tübingen: Mohr.

Hengel, M. 1989 [1961]. *The Zealots: Investigations Into the Jewish Freedom Movement in the Period from Herod I Until 70 A.D.* Trans. David Smith. Edinburgh: T & T Clark.

Hooker, Morna D. 1967. *The Son of Man in Mark*. London: SPCK.

Horbury, William. 1985. 'The Messianic Associations of "the Son of Man".' *Journal of Theological Studies* 36:34–55.

Horsley, Richard A., and John S. Hanson. 1985. *Bandits, Prophets and Messiahs: Popular Movements at the Time of Jesus*. Minneapolis: Winston Press; Edinburgh: T & T Clark.

Käsemann, Ernst. 1969 [1965]. *New Testament Questions of Today*. Trans. W. J. Montague. London: SCM.

Kellerman, Ulrich. 1979. *Auferstanden in den Himmel. 2 Makkabäer 7 und die Auferstehung der Märtyrer*. Stuttgarter Bibelstudien 95. Stuttgart: Verlag Katholisches Bibelwerk.

Koch, Klaus. 1972 [1970]. *The Rediscovery of Apocalyptic: A Polemical Work on a Neglected Area of Biblical Studies and Its Damaging Effects on Theology and Philosophy*. Trans. Margaret Kohl. Studies in Biblical Theology, vol. 2.22. London: SCM.

Landman, Leo, ed. 1979. *Messianism in the Talmudic Era*. New York: Ktav.

Loewe, R. 1981. '"Salvation" is not of the Jews.' *Journal of Theological Studies* 22:341–68.

Mack, Burton L. 1968. *A Myth of Innocence: Mark and Christian Origins*. Philadelphia: Fortress.

Moule, Charles F. D. 1977. *The Origin of Christology*. Cambridge: CUP.

Neusner, Jacob. 1987. ed., with W. S. Green and E. Frerichs. *Judaisms and Their Messiahs at the Turn of the Christian Era*. Cambridge: CUP.

Nickelsburg, George W. E. 1972. *Resurrection, Immortality and Eternal Life in Intertestamental Judaism*. Harvard Theological Studies, vol. 26. Cambridge, Mass.: Harvard U. P.

———. 1981. *Jewish Literature Between the Bible and the Mishndh*. Philadelphia: Fortress; London: SCM.

Perkins, Pheme. 1984. *Resurrection: New Testament Witness and Contemporary Reflection*. London: Geoffrey Chapman.

Rajak, Tessa. 1983. *Josephus: The Historian and His Society*. London: Duckworth; Philadelphia: Fortress.

Rofé, Alexander. 1988. 'The Onset of Sects in Postexilic Judaism: Neglected Evidence from the Septuagint, Trito-Isaiah, Ben Sira, and Malachi.' In *The Social World of Formative Christianity and Judaism: Essays in Tribute to Howard Clark Kee*, ed. Jacob Neusner, Peder Borgen, Ernest S. Frerichs, and Richard Horsley, 39–49. Philadelphia: Fortress.

Rowland, Christopher C. 1982. *The Open Heaven: A Study of Apocalyptic in Judaism and Early Christianity.* New York: Crossroad.

Sanders, E. P. 1977. *Paul and Palestinian Judaism: A Comparison of Patterns of Religion.* London: SCM; Philadelphia: Fortress.

———. 1985. *Jesus and Judaism.* London: SCM; Philadelphia: Fortress.

———. 1992. *Judaism: Practice and Belief, 63 BCE—66 CE.* London: SCM; Philadelphia: Trinity Press International.

Scholem, Gershom. 1971. *The Messianic Idea in Judaism, and Other Essays on Jewish Spirituality.* New York: Schocken.

Schürer, E. 1973–87. *The History of the Jewish People in the Age of Jesus Christ (175 B.C.—A.D. 135).* Rev. & ed. G. Vermes, F. Millar, and M. Black. 3 vols. Edinburgh: T & T Clark.

Schweitzer, Albert. 1954 [1910]. *The Quest of the Historical Jesus: A Critical Study of Its Progress from Reimarus to Wrede.* Trans. W. B. D. Montgomery. 3rd edn. London: A & C Black.

Sparks, H. F. D., ed. 1984. *The Apocryphal Old Testament.* Oxford: Clarendon Press.

Stone, Michael E. 1984. *Compendia.* Section Two. Vol. 2. *Jewish Writings of the Second Temple Period: Apocrypha, Pseudepigrapha, Qumran Sectarian Writings, Philo, Josephus.* Philadelphia: Fortress; Assen: Van Gorcum.

———. 1987. 'The Question of the Messiah in 4 Ezra.' *In Judaisms and Their Messiahs at the Turn of the Christian Era,* ed. Jacob Neusner, William S. Green, and Ernest Frerichs, 209–24. Cambridge: CUP.

———. 1990. *Fourth Ezra: A Commentary on the Book of Fourth Ezra.* Ed. Frank Moore Cross. Hermeneia. Minneapolis: Fortress.

Talmon, Shemaryahu. 1987. 'Waiting for the Messiah: The Spiritual Universe of the Qumran Covenanters.' In *Judaisms and Their Messiahs at the Turn of the Christian Era,* ed. Jacob Neusner, William S. Green, and Ernest S. Frerichs. Cambridge: CUP.

Vernes, Geza. 1987 [1962]. *The Dead Sea Scrolls in English.* 3rd edn. London: Penguin Books.

Wright, N. T. 1991a. *The Climax of the Covenant: Christ and the Law in Pauline Theology.* Edinburgh: T & T Clark; Minneapolis: Fortress.